ALASTAI
SPECIAL P

C000229970

ITALY

£14.99/$23.95

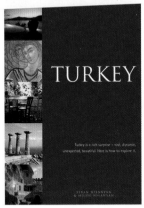

TURKEY

£11.99

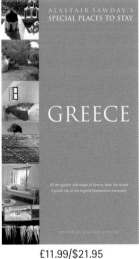

GREECE

£11.99/$21.95

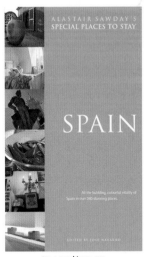

SPAIN

£14.99/$23.95

Credit card orders (free p&tp for UK orders) 01275 395431
www.specialplacestostay.com

In US: credit card orders (800) 243-0495, 9am-5pm EST,
24-hour fax (800) 820-2329 www.globepequot.com

First edition
Copyright © November 2006
Alastair Sawday Publishing Co. Ltd

Published in November 2006
Alastair Sawday Publishing,
The Old Farmyard,
Yanley Lane, Long Ashton
Bristol BS41 9LR
Tel: +44 (0)1275 395430
Fax: +44 (0)1275 393388
Email: info@specialplacestostay.com
Web: www.specialplacestostay.com

The Globe Pequot Press
P. O. Box 480, Guilford,
Connecticut 06437, USA
Tel: +1 203 458 4500
Fax: +1 203 458 4601
Email: info@globepequot.com
Web: www.globepequot.com

Design:
Caroline King
Maps & Mapping:
Maidenhead Cartographic Services Ltd

Printing:
Butler & Tanner, Frome, UK

UK Distribution:
Penguin UK, 80 Strand, London

ISBN-10: 1-901970-84-1
ISBN-13: 978-1-901970-84-5

Paper and Printing: We have sought the
lowest possible ecological 'footprint' from
the production of this book, using super-
efficient machinery, vegetable inks and
high environmental standards. Our printer is
ISO 14001-registered.

The publishers have made every effort to
ensure the accuracy of the information
in this book at the time of going to
press. However, they cannot accept
any responsibility for any loss, injury
or inconvenience resulting from the
use of information contained therein.

ALASTAIR SAWDAY'S
SPECIAL PLACES TO STAY

CROATIA

Contents

Back

Page

Photo Juraj Kopač, Croatian Tourist Board

Alastair Sawday Publishing

Our main aim is to publish beautiful guidebooks but, for us, the question of who we are is also important. For who we are shapes the books, the books shape your holidays, and thus are shaped the lives of people who own these 'special places'. So we are trying to be a little more than 'just a publishing company'.

New eco offices

In January 2006 we moved into our new eco offices. With super-insulation, underfloor heating, a wood-pellet boiler, solar panels and a rainwater tank, we have a working environment benign to ourselves and to the environment. Lighting is low-energy, dark corners are lit by sun-pipes and one building is of green oak. Carpet tiles are from Herdwick sheep in the Lake District.

Environmental & ethical policies

We make many other gestures: company cars run on gas or recycled cooking oil; kitchen waste is composted and other waste recycled; cycling and car-sharing are encouraged; the company only buys organic or local food; we don't accept web links with companies we consider unethical; we bank with the ethical Triodos Bank.

We have used recycled paper for some books but have settled on selecting paper and printing for their low energy use. Our printer is British and ISO14001-certified and together we will work to reduce our environmental impact.

In 2005 we won a Business Commitment to the Environment Award and in April 2006 we won a Queen's Award for Enterprise in the Sustainable Development category. All this has boosted our resolve to promote our green policies. Our flagship gesture, however, is carbon offsetting; we calculate our carbon emissions and plant trees to compensate. In future we will support projects overseas that plant trees or reduce carbon use.

Carbon offset

SCAD in South India supports the poorest of the poor. The money we send to offset our carbon emissions will be used to encourage village tree planting and, eventurally, low-carbon technologies. Why India? Because the money goes a long way and admin costs are very low. www.salt-of-the-earth.org.uk

Ethics

But why, you may ask, take these things so seriously? You are just a little publishing company, for heaven's sake! Well, is there any good argument for not taking them seriously? The world, by the admission of the vast majority of scientists, is in trouble. If we do not change our ways urgently we will

Who are we?

doom the planet and all its creatures – whether innocent or not – to a variety of possible catastrophes. To maintain the status quo is unacceptable. Business does much of the damage and should undo it, and provide new models.

Pressure on companies to produce Corporate Social Responsibility policies is mounting. We are trying to keep ahead of it all, yet still to be as informal and human as possible – the antithesis of 'corporate'.

The books – and a dilemma

So, we have created fine books that do good work. They promote authenticity, individuality and good local and organic food – a far cry from corporate culture. Rural economies, pubs, small farms, villages and hamlets all benefit. However, people use fossil fuel to get there. Should we aim to get our readers to offset their own carbon emissions, and the B&B and hotel owners too?

We are gradually introducing green ideas into the books: the Fine Breakfast scheme that highlights British and Irish B&B owners who use local and organic food; celebrating those who make an extra environmental effort; gently encouraging the use of public transport, cycling and walking. This year we are publishing *Green Places*

to Stay focusing on responsible travel and eco-properties around the globe.

Our Fragile Earth series

The 'hard' side of our environmental publishing is the Fragile Earth series: *The Little Earth Book, The Little Food Book* and *The Little Money Book.* They consist of bite-sized essays, polemical, hard-hitting and well researched. They are a 'must have' for anyone who seeks clarity about some of the key issues of our time. This year we have also published *One Planet Living.*

Lastly – what is special?

The notion of 'special' is at the heart of what we do, and highly subjective. We discuss this in the introduction. We take huge pleasure in finding people and places that do their own thing – brilliantly; places that are unusual and follow no trends; places of peace and beauty; people who are kind and interesting – and genuine.

We seem to have touched a nerve with thousands of readers; they obviously want to stay in special places rather than the dull corporate monstrosities that have disfigured so many of our cities and towns. Life is too short to be wasted in the wrong places. A night in a special place can be a transforming experience.

Alastair Sawday

Acknowledgements

Another first edition and a challenging project! Lisa Plumridge, Rik Mulder and their team at The Content Works have been determined, methodical, hard-working and committed – and the result is a book that is as lovely as any we have produced. We owe much to them all, and to Joseph Bindloss and Kathryn Tomasetti in particular, for the dogged and imaginative work that has gone into ferreting out such marvellous and special places.

In this office, Jo Boissevain has edited the whole book, after which it went to the production team – Julia Richardson, Allys Williams, Tom Germain, Rebecca Thomas and Rachel Coe – for final and expert finishing. Russell, our Web Producer and IT Manager, played his usual brilliantly supportive role, and the result is here for you to enjoy.

Alastair Sawday

Series Editor
Alastair Sawday

Editor
Lisa Plumridge with Rik Mulder

Editorial Director
Annie Shillito

Accounts
Bridget Bishop, Jessica Britton, Christine Buxton, Sandra Hassell, Sally Ranahan

Editorial
Jackie King, Jo Boissevain, Florence Oldfield, Maria Serrano, Rebecca Stevens, Danielle Williams

Production
Julia Richardson, Rachel Coe, Tom Germain, Rebecca Thomas, Allys Williams

Sales & Marketing & PR
Siobhán Flynn, Andreea Petre Goncalves, Sarah Bolton

Web & IT Russell Wilkinson, Chris Banks, Joe Green, Brian Kimberling

The Content Works

Writing
Joseph Bindloss, Adam Barnes, Victoria Gill

Inspections & Photography
Amanda Castleman, Victoria Gill, Arijana Goleš, Agnieszka Grunwald, Gorana Nad-Conlan, Lisa Plumridge, Rajko Radovanović, Kathryn Tomasetti, Ivan Stanić

Administration
Nina Butković, Gorana Nad-Conlan, Lisa Plumridge, Rik Mulder, Alison Radovanović, Jane Foster

www.thecontentworks.com

A word from Alastair Sawday

Having recently emerged from a system that discouraged private enterprise, Croatia is less well-endowed with great hotels and B&Bs than its western neighbours. Finding her Special Places has been especially challenging, with so much banality left over from previous regimes. Yet it is always astonishing to behold the human spirit reasserting itself after a long smothering. Croatia has become re-invigorated, and is as colourful and fascinating as anywhere in Europe. *National Geographic Magazine* declared it, in 2000, to be the most beautiful country in the world. That was brave, but says a lot. Those who go to Croatia now invariably return elated by what they have seen.

Dubrovnik and Zagreb have been compared to Prague and Krakow – and, having been cleaned, polished and restored, await the rush. The islands appear to be limitless, the sea cleaner than anywhere else in the Mediterranean, the food of a rare tastiness, the countryside spellbindingly lovely and unspoiled, the National Parks among the finest in Europe. Can this all be true? Apparently so. So if you have been nervous about going there because you didn't know where to stay, let this terrific new book be your salvation.

We have found, to our delight, Special Places all over the country: farmstays, isolated lighthouses, boutique hotels, Austro-Hungarian villas, Communist-era converted town hotels, campsites and self-catering houses in all sorts of beautiful places. We have also found many people and places with a strong focus on organic food. With our help you can get under the skin of this marvellous little country and avoid the places that might spoil your holiday, for – as we say so often – a holiday is far too precious to be spent in the wrong place. And by going to these special places you will be encouraging other good people to open their doors to visitors.

Alastair Sawday

Introduction

HISTORIC ARCHITECTURE, A GREEN GASTRONOMIC SCENE, A THRIVING CULTURAL ONE AND A TRADITION OF HOSPITALITY

Why go

Imagine a country of valleys, rivers, medieval villages and gothic palazzos. Conjure up a day exploring Roman excavations, karst gorges and red coral underworlds deep in the sea. Picture a breakfast whose ingredients were grown by your host.

Many countries would claim to be a 'land of contrasts', but Croatia's assertion is stronger than most. Teetering between Eastern and Western Europe, it sees the last vestiges of communism contrasting with a booming tourist economy. And its topographical diversity is astounding. If it had a desert, Croatia would hold a full house of the earth's landscapes. Instead you'll have to settle for rocks, islands, mountains and valleys, ski resorts and beaches, bustling cities and tiny villages.

Immensely popular with its Italian neighbours, Croatia increasingly draws visitors from farther afield. They come not only for sweeping beaches and sapphire seas but for historic architecture, a green gastronomic scene, a thriving cultural one and a tradition of hospitality.

Yet, despite all this, one of the main factors that makes Croatia special is that it has yet to succumb to mass tourism. Nature and ecology are revered and protected, the food is largely organic and local, and the countryside is unblighted. What's more, the Adriatic, peppered with over a thousand islands demanding exploration, is one of Europe's cleanest seas.

Where to go

Any first-time visitor to Croatia is likely to make for the winding strip of coastline that is Dalmatia, a beguiling blend of cities, islands, landscape and sea. The majesty

Photo above Hotel Vinarija, entry 160
Photo left House Ivela, entry 21

of millennia-old towns such as Dubrovnik, Split, Zadar and Trogir is matched by the tranquillity of islands such as Mljet, Vis, Hvar and Brač. Here too are the wondrous Krka Falls and the striking karst landscape of the Northern Velebit National Park.

In the northwest of the country, the hilltop towns, valleys and pristine coastline of Istria are gaining increasing attention. The cobblestoned cluster of towns made up of Višnjan, Motovun, Grožnjan and Buje are as much of a joy to approach as they are to meander. Seaside landmarks such as Pula, Labin, Poreč and Rovinj still carry the hallmarks of their historic pasts.

Photo Villa Dubrava, entry 55

The northernmost tip from which to explore the islands, Kvarner – the 'gateway to the National Parks' – is the area between Istria, Dalmatia and inland Croatia. Embracing Gorski Kotar, with its sweeping river canyons and skiing, the Kvarner Gulf stretches out to the islands of Rab, Krk and Cres. The genteel neighbouring resorts of Lovran and Opatija still display the Hapsburg hallmarks of their Austro-Hungarian heritage, while the waterfall-laden beauty of the Plitvice Lakes is arresting.

Croatia's capital, Zagreb, has special places in this book, alongside a number of lesser-known inland pearls. The country's largest city has a Viennese feel, with national museums, theatres, galleries, festivals and a thriving music scene. The beguiling towns of Samobor and Varaždin each lie within reach, while Slavonia's Mount Papuk is memorable, looming high over the province's gentle flatlands.

When to go

In July and August you are most likely to come across tourists drawn to the summer sun. Prices escalate along with the temperatures; these hover around the 30-degree mark and often surpass it. Autumn is an excellent time to visit: the crowds thin, the temperatures drop, and the sea is still warm. It's also one of the most fertile times for the country's agriculture, so for those wishing to explore the interior, September to November is a superb time to visit.

Don't dismiss winter: during the quietest period in the tourist calendar, winter sports erupt as prices fall – sometimes dramatically. Sun-worshippers should head south, where some islands enjoy almost year-round sunshine.

Spring's prices are also considerably lower than summer's, nature blooms and Croatia is relatively tourist-free. South of Split, temperatures remain constant and warm. By May, the coastline is heating up.

Getting there and getting around
Most country hotels are happy to pick you up on arrival from the nearest airport or station.

If you're planning to travel to the interior, a car is something of a necessity. Buses tend to be timed to coincide with school runs: first thing in the morning and mid-afternoon. For long-distance bus journeys from larger cities, services are relatively cheap and frequent. You need to pay a luggage fee to the ticket collector outside. Some bus stations have details online; Zagreb's information is at www.akz.hr

Photo Ivo Pervan, Croatian Tourist Board

Trains can be a charming and inexpensive way of seeing the countryside; station locations can, however, be eccentric. See Croatia Railways' website for all you need to know: www.hznet.hr

Croatia's geography being what it is, an aeroplane is the easiest way to travel long distances. The flight from Zagreb to Dubrovnik takes an hour; the bus takes 24 hours. Croatia Airlines has frequent domestic flights.

The islands are served by ferries. To get from the north to the south of the Adriatic coast takes around 24 hours. To get from Croatia to Italy and back look at www.sem-marina.hr; Jadrolinia Ferry Company serves all the main routes: www.jadrolinija.hr. Island ferries run from the major cities to the islands all year round, but are far more frequent during the summer.

Introduction

Taxis tend to charge exorbitant prices; most locals have their own cars and don't use taxis. Off-season it may be possible to negotiate a price. For more reasonable tariffs, most cities have a Citycar service, similar to minicabs; prices are around half those of a taxi. Be warned: taxis are scarce in the countryside.

The obvious way to travel around Croatia is by car, and the major hire companies operate there. Be aware that you need a full British driving licence to hire a car or scooter. Croatians drive on the right. For details on laws and regulations, look at the Croatian Automobile Association website: www.hak.hr

Airports and airlines
British Airways, Croatia Airlines, Flyglobespan, Excel Airways, GB Airways and Wizzair fly direct from various British airports to Croatian destinations including Pula, Zagreb, Split, Dubrovnik and Rijeka. Ryanair also flies direct to Ljubljana in Slovenia, Trieste in Italy and Ancona in Italy. From Ljubljana and Trieste you can take a coach, train or shared airport taxi to Istria, while Ancona has frequent ferry connections to the Dalmatian coast.

Communications
The country code for Croatia is 385. Mobile numbers begin 099, 098 (VIP, affiliated to Vodafone) or 091.

To call the UK from Croatia dial 00 44, then drop the first 0 from the local area code (eg. central London calls will start 00 44 207).

Be warned that hotels, like hotels everywhere, often charge inflated rates for international calls.

Tourist offices
Every town has a tourist office. Along with your hosts, these will be your best source of advice on local customs, holidays, festivals, places to visit, shops, restaurants, transport and opening times.
These are the national and regional branches:

Croatian National Tourist Information: www.croatia.hr

Dubrovnik:
Cvijete Zuzorić 1/I, p.p. 259, 2001 Dubrovnik. Tel: 020 324 999. www.visitdubrovnik.hr

Istria:
Pionirska 1, 52440 Poreč. Tel: 052 452 797. Or: Forum 3, 52100, Pula. Tel: 052 214 201. www.istra.hr

Slavonia:
Županijska 7, 34000 Požega. Tel: 034 272 505. www.tzzps.hr

Kvarner:
N. Tesle 2, p.p. 52, 51410 Opatija. Tel: 051 272 988. www.kvarner.hr

Introduction

The Šibenik region, Dalmatia:
www.summernet.hr/county-sibenik-knin

Split and the Dalmatian Coast: Prilaz
brače Kaliterna 10/l, p.p. 430. 21000
Split. Tel: 021 490 032.
www.dalmatia.hr and
www.visitsplit.com

Zadar:
Sv Leopolda B. Mandića 1. 23000
Zadar. Tel: 023 315 107.
www.zadar.hr

Zagreb:
Preradovićeva 42, 10000 Zagreb. Tel:
01 4873 665. www.tzzz.hr or
www.zagrebtouristinfo.hr

What makes a place special?
The notion of 'special' is of course
subjective – and so is the portfolio
of places in this book. Each place is
different, chosen not because of star
ratings or whether it has room
service, lifts, fitness rooms or
children's facilities. Special is that
feeling you get when you walk
through the door.

Individuality is the key. Each of the
properties featured in this book has
something that makes it stand out.
It may be to do with the style of the
building or the level of care shown
by the host, it may be the setting,
the cooking, the history; often, a
place will embrace all of these. A
converted olive press, where wooden
beams shelter the head and each
room tells a story, is special.
Scrambled eggs with truffles served
on gingham tablecloths by an open
fire is special. Or a farm where
cockerels wake you and owls hoot
you to sleep.

We place a big emphasis on an
owner's approach to food and
particularly appreciate those
who have an ecological or social
conscience. And we do not believe
this special quality has to come
with a high price tag. Each place in
this book is special, be it an
eco-village where your shower is
a river or a baroque palace where
the cotton count of your linen is
tailored upon request.

Photo Josip Madračevič, Croatian Tourist Board

How to use this book

Prices

Prices vary considerably according to when you go, dropping in winter and escalating in July and August. From a €5-a-tent tariff to a bed for €300 per night, the prices in this book refer to the cost of a double room based on two people sharing. As a rough guide for a majority of places, expect to pay around €60 in high season and €40 in low.

We quote some prices in euros, others in kuna (Kn), the national currency. We state which currency the hotel prefers, but almost everywhere will accept both. Taxes are not included in our prices, and many places will levy a small charge, usually a couple of euros. Be aware that some places add a fee for heating and electricity during the colder months; if you are the only people staying in February you may have to carry the brunt of the entire building's heating. Do check.

All but the most luxurious hotels and B&Bs will refuse credit cards and many will want a deposit, particularly during high season. This is usually paid via bank transfer. Also know that prices don't always reflect levels of comfort – we feature ancient palaces that charge as little as €30 per night – and that hotel rates inland are much lower.

Photo Hotel Vestibul Palace, entry 88

That said, rates compare favourably with just about anywhere in the Mediterranean – even taking into account the most expensive areas of Zagreb and Southern Dalmatia.

Types of property

Croatia's non-package tour approach to tourism is reflected in this book. Choose a lighthouse in the Adriatic where you can join the local fishermen for the morning's catch; a five-star palace in Dubrovnik's Old Town; a working farm where breakfast milk comes fresh from the cow; a watermill on a nature reserve where the river serenades you to sleep; a chic rock stars' hideaway.

One relic of the communist era is the rule that hotels must show guest passports to the local police to validate who's in town, so be prepared to part with your passport on check-in.

Introduction

Many in this book are as lavish as a hotel, but are unlikely to have maids to collect your laundry, and the concierge may be the owner's son. Stancija Negrićani is one such example: a luxuriously rustic B&B with antique-filled bedrooms and a lovely pool.

Our hotels cover just about every type – but not those sprawling complexes with 500 rooms, pool volleyball and an array of breakfast and lunchtime buffets. Some are boutique hotels; most are independently run. They have been chosen because they have character, pleasing interiors, warm service and fabulous settings: from Palmižana Meneghello (an idyllic collection of modernist stone bungalows set in a herb garden on a private bay) to Palača Dešković, a stately mansion run by a Countessa on the island of Brač, to the Art Nouveau splendour of Zagreb's Hotel Palace.

The majority of our self-catering apartments have been selected because their owners do more than simply hand over a set of keys. Some have owners or staff on site who will make breakfast should you wish, tell you about the local attractions and even share supper time with you; others may not be staffed but are beautifully sited (Villa Jezero overlooks Mljet's breathtaking National Park) or regally appointed (Villa San Giovanni's endless corridors ooze Hapsburg charm).

What marks a B&B out from a hotel? A B&B (or guest house or *pansion*, as they are sometimes called) will probably be smaller in scale, will not necessarily have a lounge, room service or pool, and have fewer staff.

A few places serve no meals at all, but may still be quite luxurious. Base Sobe in Split is built into the Roman walls of the Temple of Jupiter, while the Ilički Plac apartments are in a grand Zagreb building overlooking one of the city's main markets. Our villas range from simple village homes with open fires to state-of-the-art mansions with swimming pools, jacuzzis, cleaners, caretakers and cooks. Those villas

Photo above Chris Lucas
Photo right Quentin Craven

without staff have kitchens or kitchenettes and a restaurant nearby. FromStonehouse, a cluster of restored stone houses on the hills outside Jelsa, with their underfloor heating and ozone pools, to Humac House, a lovingly restored cottage in an abandoned village on Hvar Island where your sole neighbours are sheep, each property has its individual style.

Bedrooms and bathrooms

Nearly all the bedrooms in this book have an en suite bath or shower. Bedrooms vary hugely – from basic with a bed that the host's grandfather was born in to cutting-edge contemporary furnished with 20th-century

antiques. Owners often call rooms with two beds pushed together doubles – important to know if you prefer twins, or insist on no seam down the centre of the bed. Many bathrooms are basically equipped and have a shower not a bath (even in the swishest hotels); others are opulent with state-of-the-art wet rooms, saunas and jacuzzis. Remember to bring an English adaptor if you're carrying electrical equipment; these are mystifyingly hard to come by.

Meals

Croatia's culinary offerings are a mix of regional specialities and seafood. Every fish restaurant along the coast serves lobster, John Dory, squid, oysters and red mullet. Istrian cuisine has a particularly strong Italian influence; inland, expect a more Central European feel.

Croatia is unusual in the variety of its produce. Great value is set by organic and locally sourced ingredients: some hosts will fish your supper time catch themselves. Other places are happy for you to help yourselves from the produce from their vegetable patch or orchard, choose wine from their cellars, invite you to milk their goats, pick their grapes or hunt for truffles in the forest. Some hotels and B&Bs have won awards for their wine and olive oil; others run fine restaurants.

Photo above Agroturizam Matijasič, entry 20
Photo right Kado Resort & Spa, entry 69

Villa Wolff invented the phenomenon of gastro-hopping, where you book a table at a different restaurant every night, while the eco village of Zrno runs cookery courses with a strict macrobiotic ethos. The inimitable menu of Valsabbion treats you to eight courses of Istrian haute cuisine served on crockery crafted from mirrors and fragments of antique urns.

In many guest houses breakfast is not standard, so you need to order in advance. The spread will be either continental or regional. Some places will gladly cook you dinner as well, if you ask; others prepare picnic hampers for a day out.

Photo Damir Fabijanić, Croatian Tourist Board

Where breakfast is not included we give a per person price; for lunch and dinner too. Self-catered properties may, in addition to a kitchen or kitchenette, have a barbecue in the grounds, a summer kitchen or an open fire; even a *konoba* (tavern) on site. Others come with a chef who will cook for you. When there is no dining on site, the distance to the nearest restaurant is given.

Note that apartments and studios have a legal requirement to contain a kitchen or kitchenette; 'rooms' do not. Check when booking though, as some owners are not keen on guests cooking meals every night and may even withhold crockery and implements; minimal use may be expected.

Dates closed
You have nothing to worry about in summer: many hoteliers earn their entire annual income during these months. Some properties stay open all year round, a few are closed through the winter, others have idiosyncratic closing periods in low season. We've indicated opening and closing dates for each place – but always check if you're visiting outside the peak months.

Directions
Use as a rough guide, check with booking, and always travel with a

good map. Note that some street names are followed by 'bb' eg. 'Pantan bb': this in Croatia is the equivalent of zero and stands for 'bez broja' (without a number). Note too that the so-called 'Istrian Y' refers to motorway Route 8 and the A9, its two stretches meeting at Kanfanar in south-central Istria.

Booking

Although Croatia is switching on to the wonders of email, some owners prefer the fax. A phone call is probably the fastest way of securing a booking, though in low season it could be a problem contacting some B&Bs.

Tipping

Tipping is common in restaurants; add around ten per cent to the bill. Tipping taxis is not necessary; you should, however, round up the bill.

Quick reference indices

The quick reference section at the back of this book will direct you to places suitable for wheelchair users or with a pleasant outside space; with bicycles to borrow or a short stroll from the beach.

Subscriptions

Owners pay to appear in this guide. Their fee goes towards the high costs of inspecting and producing an all-colour book

and maintaining a sophisticated website. We only include places that we like and find special for one reason or another. It is not possible for anyone to buy their way onto these pages.

Internet

www.specialplacestostay.com has online pages for all the special places featured here and from all our other books – around 5,000 in total. There's a searchable database, a taster of the write-ups and colour photos. And look out for our dedicated self-catering web site, www.specialescapes.co.uk. For more details, see the back of the book.

Photo Humac House, entry 102

Disclaimer

We make no claims to pure objectivity in choosing our Special Places. They are here because we like them. Our opinions and tastes are ours alone and this book is a statement of them; we hope that you will share them. We have done our utmost to get our facts right and we apologise unreservedly for any errors that may have crept in. We do not check such things as fire alarms, swimming pool security or any other regulation with which owners of properties receiving paying guests should comply. This is the responsibility of the owners.

Feedback

Feedback from you is invaluable and we always act upon comments, which may be sent by letter or email to info@sawdays.co.uk. Or you can visit our web site and write to us from there. With your help and our own inspections we can maintain our reputation for dependability – and do bear with us at busy times; it's difficult to respond immediately.

Poor reports are followed up with the owners in question: we need to hear both sides of the story. Really bad reports lead to incognito visits, after which we may exclude a place. As a general rule, do mention any problems that may arise to the relevant people during your stay;

they should want to resolve them on the spot.

Owners are informed when we receive substantially positive reports about them, and recommendations are followed up with inspection visits where appropriate. If your recommendation leads us to include a place, you receive a free copy of the edition in which it first appears.

So tell us if your stay has been a joy or not, if the atmosphere was great or stuffy, whether the owners or staff were cheery or bored. We aim to celebrate human kindness, fine architecture, real food, history and landscape, and hope that these books may be a passport to memorable experiences.

Photo Hotel Kanajt, entry 71
Photo Ivo Pervan, Croatian Tourist Board

General map

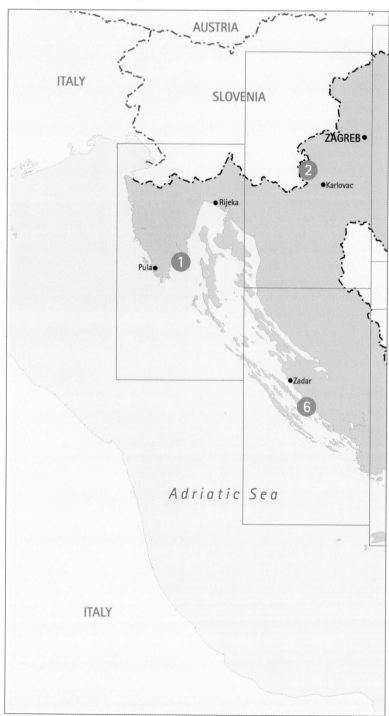

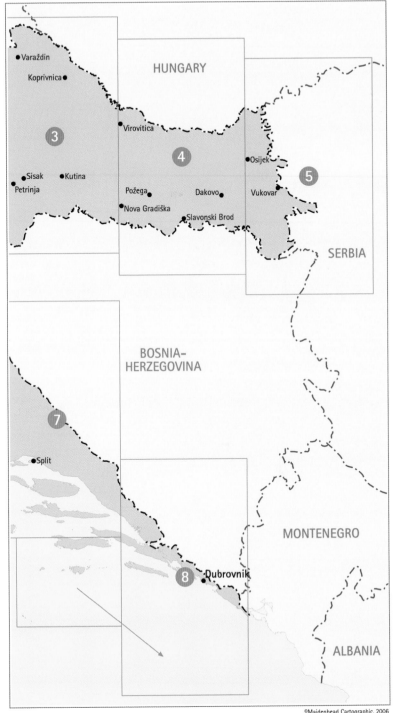

Map 1

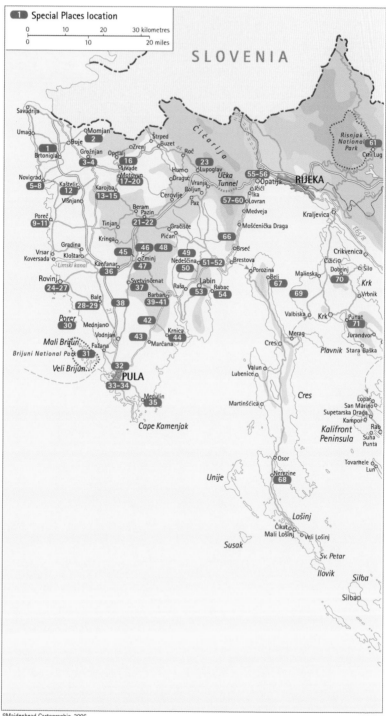

Map 2

29

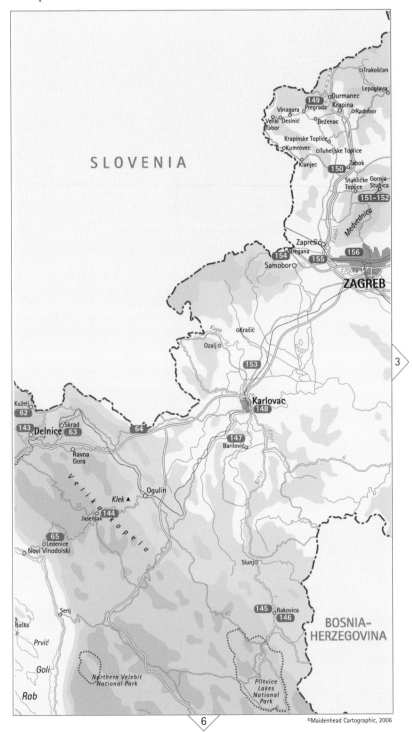

Map 3

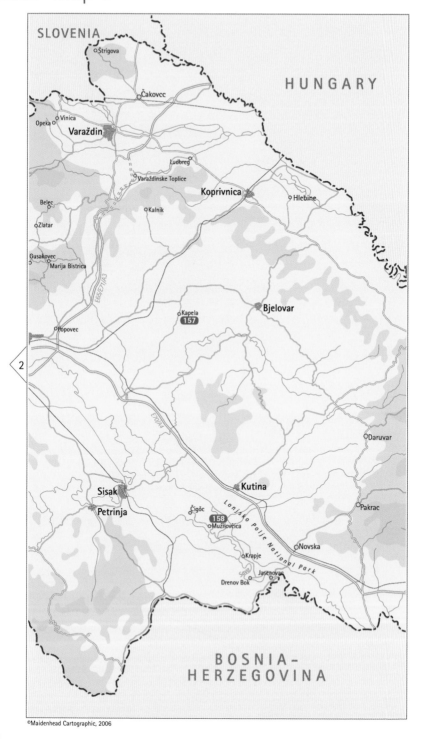

SLOVENIA

HUNGARY

Štrigova

Čakovcc

Opeka Vinica

Varaždin

Ludbreg

Varaždinske Toplice

Koprivnica

Hlebine

Belec

Kalnik

Zlatar

Gusakovec

Marija Bistrica

E65/E71/A3

Kapela

Bjelovar

157

Popovec

2

E70/A1

Daruvar

Kutina

Lonjsko Polje National Park

Sisak

Čigôc

Petrinja

158

Pakrac

Mužilovčica

Novska

Krapje

Sava

Jasenovac

Drenov Bok

BOSNIA-
HERZEGOVINA

Map 4

31

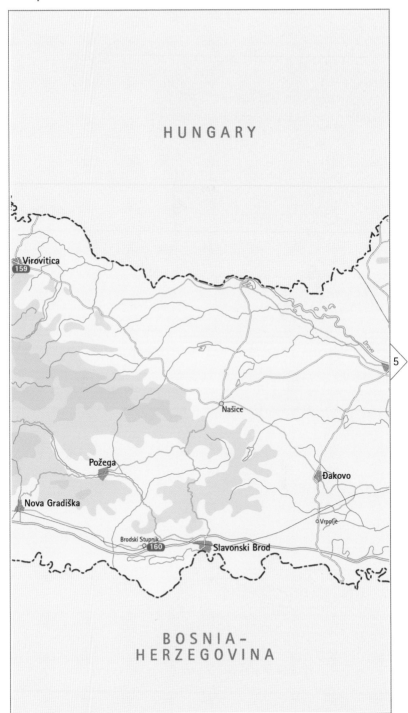

Map 5

HUNGARY

Danube

Kopački
Rit
National
Park

161

Bilje °Kopačevo

Osijek

162

4

SERBIA

Vukovar

Šarengrad °

Ilok °

BOSNIA–
HERZEGOVINA

Map 6

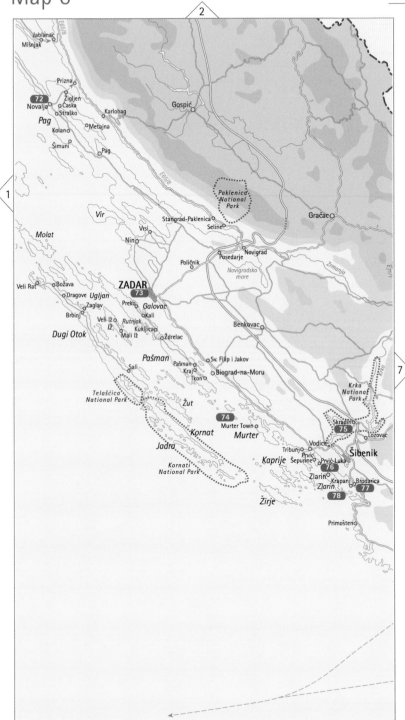

BOSNIA–
HERZEGOVINA

Knin

Manojlovački
slapovi

Drniš   Otavice

6

Sinj

Kaštel-
Gomilica
Kaštel-Lukšić   Kozjak   Kaštel-
Kaštel-Stari   Sućurac
Kaštel-Novi   Klis
83   Salona
79-82 Trogir
84   85   SPLIT
       86-89   Podstrana
Čiovo   90
              Duće Omiš
           Dugi Rat   E65/8   Zadvarje
91   Brela
Sutivan 92 Supetar   Tppići   Biokovo Nature Park
        Splitska   Brač Baška Voda Bast Sv.
        Škrip   Promajna Jure
Šolta   Pučišće   Krvavica
      Milna   93   Makar
        Blacao Vidova gora   Kotišina
Murvica   Sumartin Makarska
        Bol 94-95   Zlatni rat   Tučepi
                              Podgora
98-99 Stari Grad 97 Vboska
Hvar   Milna Sv. Jelsa 101   Igrane
96   Zaraće Nikola 100 Humac
        Dubovica Sv. Nedjelja Zavala 102   Drvenik
Palmižana   Zaostrog
                  Hvar   Sućuraj

      Kut
Komiža Vis   Ploćica
103   Rukavac   105   Trpanj
    104   Nakovanj 106
Vis   Proizd   Viganj Kučište

Imotski

Vopad
Gubavica

Cetina

Map 8

35

Istria: 'the new Riviera'

The high country, up in the northwest, is celebrated for its landscape – one of Croatia's richest. Ringed by a pristine coastline and filled with lush valleys overlooked by hilltop towns, Istria has something for everyone. Historians fall in love with the interior, a treasure house of pre-Christian, Roman and medieval heritage, seekers of rural seclusion are happy up in the hills, while the coastal mansions of seafarers have been converted into boutique billets for the chic.

Nature lovers should make for the Brijuni Islands. John F Kennedy, Sophia Loren, Queen Elizabeth II and President Tito are among those to have been enchanted by the scenery of the archipelago that forms Istria's only national park.

Motovun is the jewel of Istria's medieval towns, crowning a green hilltop in a region dotted with lofty hill towns. It is an architectural feast of winding, UNESCO-protected cobblestone streets lined with delicatessens and truffle restaurants. Film enthusiasts should make the trip in late July for the Film Festival.

During the 1960s artists began to reclaim the derelict houses of Grožnjan, a fortified hilltop town. Today, sea and valley views peep between the old stone houses, independent galleries pop up on every corner and the sound of music wafts over the streets – particularly in summer, when the town welcomes the summer music school.

Novigrad, on the northwest coast, was a thriving Roman port, but the town is defined by the fortified Byzantine wall that curls around parts of the seafront. Renaissance mansions and Venetian squares are strung out along a curving spit of land, protecting a pretty marina and fishing port lined with seafood restaurants.

Further south, Rovinj is the pearl of the coastline – a tight knot of alleyways rising to a towering 17th-century cathedral. The medieval old town is fetching indeed, the tall steeple of Sv Eufemija looming over the city like a beacon. Offshore is the century-old shipwreck of the Baron Gautsch, one of Croatia's main diving attractions.

Seaside town Pula is Istria's busiest resort but its Roman amphitheatre is one of the most perfectly preserved in the world. Sun-seekers drift along the coast to the sandy bay at Pješčana uvala, a sedate seaside resort renowned for its marina and seafood restaurants.

Perched on a clifftop, medieval Labin scatters itself around a grand open square, its tiny lanes dotted with galleries and independent craft shops. North of Labin are the often snow-covered peaks of the Učka massif, the highest mountain range in Istria; on the seashore below is the sleepy seaside retreat of Rabac.

Istria

Hotel San Rocco

Srednja ulica 2, Brtonigla, 52474 Istria

One of Istria's most charming hotels, the San Rocco lies in the far north, its remoteness adding to its allure. The Italian influence is tangible – even the name of the village, Brtonigla, conjures up images of pasta infused with truffles. Italian is still the first language of the Fernetich family, who have restored the stately buildings and Romanesque-style arches and tiles to their original splendour. The approach is enticing, through olive groves and lawns strewn with ruins. Bedrooms, intimate and snug, topped by a gantry of ancient wooden beams, have small shuttered windows, shining pale boards and beds dressed in sky blues, maraschino pinks and meadow greens. Furnishings are a mix of old and new – antique chests, iron balustrades, cream lamps. Outside is a lovely swimming pool surrounded by teak loungers and tables. You breakfast on Istrian delicacies – organic fruit, wind-cured ham, sheep's cheese – on the surrounding terrace overlooking the grounds. The restaurant serves the dishes that made the region famous: truffles, game and pasta, helped along by fine vintages from the cellar.

rooms	12 doubles.
price	€123–€149. Singles less 35%.
meals	Lunch & dinner around €40.
closed	Never.
directions	From Pula, westwards dir. Kopar (SLO); 70km, then exit Nova Vas; Brtonigla 3km.

Hotel

	Teo Fernetich
tel	+385 (0)52 725 000
fax	+385 (0)52 725 026
email	info@san-rocco.hr
web	www.san-rocco.hr

Map 1 Entry 1

Villa Kluni
Kluni 92, Momjan, 52462 Istria

This is the domain of Alistair Stephen, a Scotsman through and through, who fell in love with this delicious corner of Istria while working in Croatia. A passionate biker, proud of his roots, he has beautified this traditional stone house in hilltop Momjan with Scottish antiques and British quirks: on top of the open fireplace is a replica of Antony Gormley's dramatic 'Angel of the North'. Interesting details abound in your arched and columned home. Upstairs: a study, a roomy terrace and bedrooms with sweeping pinewood floors, classic oak dressers, white muslin, striking stone arches and hefty overhead beams. The house is rented as a self-contained villa with three tidy bedrooms, one en suite. In summer, the large pool is all yours, while the summer kitchen with original fireplace encourages long, languorous lunches in the peaceful flower-filled garden. All around are fields and forests that are home to rabbits, birds and deer: unspoiled countryside is a footstep away. Further afield are vineyards, beautiful medieval towns and festivals aplenty.

rooms	House for 6.
price	9,500 Kn-26,000 Kn per week.
meals	Self-catering. Restaurant in Kremenje, 1km.
closed	Never.
directions	From Umag, 14km east to Buje, then 3km northeast. Detailed directions on booking.

	Alistair Stephen	Self-catering
mobile	+385 (0)91 144 4001	
email	alistairstephen@yahoo.co.uk	

Map 1 Entry 2

Pintur

Mate Gorjana 9, Grožnjan, 52429 Istria

Set on a tiny knoll in Grožnjan, wrapped in a maze of cobblestone streets, Pintur takes its title from Ivan Černeka's family nickname – barrelmaker – and is appealingly rustic. Guest rooms are in the old stone house, above a *konoba* serving Istrian delicacies. At the back is a pretty garden where guests drawn to Grožnjan by artistic pursuits can draw or paint. The Pintur experience is for those who appreciate the arts but prefer to stay with unpretentious, friendly hosts. You'll taste fine Istrian cooking – al dente pasta with truffles, richly flavoured game and wild asparagus – and everything here is locally sourced. Grožnjan town is one of the loveliest in Istria, and a hive of creativity. The art scene kicked off in the 1960s, when artists began to renovate the derelict medieval houses as summer studios. There are all sorts of artistic events, particularly in summer, when Grožnjan comes alive with the strains of violins, brass and woodwind from the summer music school. So, the narrow Venetian lanes now teem with galleries and small shops. Glimpsed between are fabulous views that tumble over rolling hills and deep, green valleys.

rooms	2 doubles.
price	300 Kn. Singles 200 Kn.
meals	Breakfast 40 Kn.
	Lunch & dinner 35 Kn-120 Kn.
closed	Never.
directions	From Pula, 80km north towards Trieste. In centre of Grožnjan.

Restaurant with rooms

Ivan Černeka

tel	+385 (0)52 776 397
mobile	+385 (0)98 568 188
fax	+385 (0)52 776 015
email	ivan.cerneka@pu.t-com.hr

Map 1 Entry 3

Radanić Hotel
Radanići bb, Grožnjan, 52429 Istria

On the top of a hill surrounded by fruit trees, sprawling vineyards and thick brush, the Radanić Hotel harks back to Istria's golden age. In an area filled with peaks and knolls, the hotel oversees green hills tumbling down to rivers that lead to the blue waters of the Adriatic. Chef Remigio's culinary prowess draws Istrians from far and wide with home-grown ingredients and flavours that many people remember from childhood. Even the olive oil is pressed from fruit of nearby groves. Truffles pulled from the surrounding forests, game caught in the woods below and organic vegetables grown on family land can all be savoured on the sprawling hotel terrace, where the views are an instant antidote to the stresses of city life. Inside, the hotel has a rural charm – stone walls, saloon-style lanterns overhead and hunting trophies on the walls. Bedrooms are small and functional, decorated in familiar Istrian style. Manager Ljerka travelled the world, learning her trade, before returning home. She will take personal care of you during your stay, and guide you towards the loveliest corners of this area of Istria.

rooms	6 doubles.
price	250 Kn-360 Kn.
meals	Lunch & dinner 160 Kn.
closed	Never.
directions	From Buje 6km southeast to Krasica; 3km east to Grožnjan. Detailed directions on booking.

	Ljerka Hubert	Hotel
tel	+385 (0)52 776 353	
mobile	+385 (0)98 496 931	

Map 1 Entry 4

Makin

Saini 2a, Novigrad, 52466 Istria

Your host Sergio Makin, a former star of the Yugoslavian national football team, turned to hospitality after hanging up his boots from the restaurant ceiling: they dangle there still today. Crammed with boars' heads, wooden pails, landscape paintings and football trophies, this hotel-taverna is rated among the top 100 restaurants in Croatia. Tuck into freshly unearthed Istrian truffles in season, and fish and spiny langoustines from Novigrad harbour all year round. Several generations of the family help to run the hotel and the welcome is outstanding. These are the kind of intuitive hosts who are there the second you need them, and are quietly invisible when you don't. The hotel is bright, modern and uncluttered, more a place for families with simple tastes than for lovers of history and flamboyant design. However, the interior is touched with greenery, the grounds are supremely verdant and some bedrooms have balconies looking towards the distant ocean, refreshed by sea breezes. As for the harbour, it is flanked by monumental Byzantine city walls and some wonderful Renaissance towers.

Hotel

rooms	15: 5 doubles, 10 triples.
price	€40–€100.
	Singles €40–€55.
	Half-board extra €10 p.p.
meals	Dinner from €11.
closed	Never.
directions	From Novigrad centre 1km, on main road to Umag. Detailed directions on booking.

Daniel Makin

tel	+385 (0)52 757 714
mobile	+385 (0)98 434 699
fax	+385 (0)52 757 714
email	hotel-makin@mail.inet.hr
web	www.istra.com/makin

Map 1 Entry 5

Villa Paolija

Paolija 19b, Novigrad, 52466 Istria

The gleaming three-wheeled bike parked outside the palm-tree fronted chalet provides the first clue: Zlatko Blažić is a man who loves the open road. Once a travelling salesman, he has swapped his smart saloon for a motorbike – perfect for exploring the back lanes of Istria. One of life's enthusiasts, he likes nothing more than to crack open a beer at the end of the day and get stuck into some deep debate. The house lies at the end of a village overlooking woods and meadows. Chickens cluck in the yard, two century-old oak trees shade the terrace. Inside are two huge apartments, simply styled with basic kitchens and bedrooms decorated in plain white. The private terraces, too, are vast; plonk yourself in a chair and gaze on rural bliss – the house is surrounded by fields and woods, gambolling rabbits and darting pheasants. Villa Paolija is in a superb spot: nearby is the stately Venetian port of Novigrad, whose beaches are backed by a string of excellent seafood restaurants, while inland are the area's famous wine roads and the romantic towns of Brtonigla and Buje.

rooms	2 apartments for 4.
price	€45–€70.
meals	Self-catering. Restaurants in Novigrad, 3km.
closed	Never.
directions	From Novigrad, 2km northeast. Right at Bužinija; 1km east. Detailed directions on booking.

Self-catering

	Zlatko Blažić
tel	+385 (0)52 758 346
mobile	+385 (0)98 9515 410
email	zlatko.blazic@pu.htnet.hr
web	www.villa-paolija.com

Map 1 Entry 6

Torci 18

Torci 34, Novigrad, 52466 Istria

The family has been producing virgin olive oils for generations in the hills around Mandrač – recalling the years of Roman rule when only the oil from the small triangle of villages around the port was deemed good enough to grace the tables of the emperors. The gastronomic tradition lives on at the family restaurant, tucked beneath the sea wall in Novigrad, on the bulge of land running out to the marina. Tuck into fresh mullet and octopus caught in rocky coves around the islands, vegetables from the family land, and award-winning malvasia wines. This is very much a family taverna, all dark wood furniture and polished walnut boards, and arches that mirror the fortress grandeur of the city. In the courtyard is an old stone olive press – the *torci:* a memento of the family business. Bedrooms, with parquet floors and homely furniture, are above and behind and back onto the crenellated city walls. The sea is metres from the door. The family is hands-on, everyone is looked after, bathrooms shine, windows look onto city walls or the sea, and the olive oil is among the best in the world.

Restaurant with rooms

rooms	12 twins.
price	380 Kn–464 Kn.
	Triple 540 Kn–620 Kn.
	Half-board extra 100 Kn p.p.
meals	Lunch & dinner 90 Kn–175 Kn.
closed	Never.
directions	From Novigrad Mandrač (marina), 100m south through Passage Venezia; right to Gradska Vrata; left into Torci.

Kristian Beletić

tel	+385 (0)52 757 799
fax	+385 (0)52 757 174
email	torci@nautico.hr
web	www.torci18.hr

Map 1 Entry 7

Hotel Nautica

Sv Antona 15, Novigrad, 52466 Istria

Seventh-century Novigrad was fortified under the Venetians, who transported oak from Motovun via its port. Quieter than other west-coast resorts, this is all set to change as Novigrad's spanking new marina puts it on the nautical map. Hotel Nautica – naturally enough – presides over it all. The exterior is bold, burgundy, contemporary, with a large, lamp-filled terrace for people-watching. Inside is extreme comfort with a nautical theme. There's mahogany and leather in abundance, and bedrooms are capacious and plush with sensuous ivory bedspreads, smooth wine carpets, elegant cream curtains and framed antique maps. The lounge bar is the place for a mid-morning cappuccino and a White Russian at six; in the restaurant, chef Marin Rendić serves Istrian and Mediterranean dishes. As if this weren't quite enough pampering for one holiday, the wellness centre trumpets a sauna, Turkish bath and therapies. So, a place for yachties, celebrities and the Raybans set – but also a great spot from which to delve into the city's architectural riches.

rooms	42: 38 doubles, 4 suites for 2.
price	€130–€180. Suite €175–€340.
meals	Lunch & dinner from €20.
closed	Never.
directions	500m from Novigrad city centre. Directions on booking.

	Suzana Vrtičević
tel	+385 (0)52 600 400
fax	+385 (0)52 600 490
email	info@nauticahotels.com
web	www.nauticahotels.com

Hotel

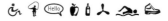

Map 1 Entry 8

Castle Isabella
Otok Sv Nikola, Poreč, 52440 Istria

A true beauty, Castle Isabella stands proud in a park on the island of Sv Nikola, surrounded by centuries-old pine and cedar trees. Stately and rarified, it was once the preserve of the noble Polestini family, their hometown of Poreč a few minutes' boat ride across the bay. Interiors are classically Italianate, walls are adorned with portraits of regally dressed ancestors, and ceilings seem to stretch up forever; richly upholstered antique furniture fills the rooms, marble floors create a mood of Italian whimsy, and the tall windows in the best bedrooms gaze out over the sea. The stillness of Sv Nikola and its shimmering waters are in bold contrast to the busy charm of Poreč, one of Istria's oldest ports with Roman origins, now a lively seaside town and a popular stop for weekenders. Those too noble to leave the island will find plenty to do to fill their stay, in addition to enjoying Istrian pasta, stone-oven baked meat and ocean-fresh seafood at the sister hotel. The wine list is predominantly local and dinners are often themed to reflect the latest seasonal and regional delicacies. *Minimum stay three nights.*

Hotel

rooms	11: 4 doubles, 3 triples, 4 quadruples.
price	€48–€131. Triples €63–€179. Quadruples €90–€256. Buffet half-board extra €6 p.p.
meals	Lunch & dinner at sister hotel in island, 200m; à la carte from €75 for 2.
closed	November-April.
directions	From seafront in Poreč, take Riviera boat to Sv Nikola island.

Reservations

tel	+385 (0)52 465 100
fax	+385 (0)52 451 440
email	reservations-porec@valamar.com
web	www.valamar.com

Map 1 Entry 9

Residence Jadran

Obala Maršala Tita 15, Poreč, 52440 Istria

The white canvas of old sailing ships moored in Poreč's harbour billows outside, and the rooms in this historic building speak of a time when weary seafarers rested in its beds. On the promenade overlooking the green Island of Sv Nikola, the Residence Jadran is a small and elegant hotel housed in a graceful seafront mansion. Built during the rule of the Austro-Hungarian Empire, it has many noble hallmarks: ceilings that soar, arches that frame portraits of grand public spaces and windows that gaze wistfully onto the marina beyond. Vast bedrooms have an understated appeal: tall white walls with dark picture rails, herringbone floors, fluttering white curtains and balcony views of ocean blue. The old centre, one of Istria's most charming, lies close by, and the gothic architecture will delight you. The maze-like streets, laid in Roman times, invite you to explore galleries, museums, palaces, exhibitions, while the UNESCO-protected sixth-century Euphrasian Basilica is ever present on the horizon. Retreat to the evening peace of the Jadran's gentle section of the town's waterfront. *Minimum stay three nights.*

rooms	22: 10 doubles, 2 singles, 10 triples.	
price	€32–€104. Single €22–€52. Triple €40–€154. Buffet half-board extra €6 p.p.	
meals	Lunch & dinner at sister hotel 150m; à la carte from €75 for 2.	
closed	November–April.	
directions	On Poreč promenade. Detailed directions on booking.	

	Reservations	Hotel
tel	+385 (0)52 465 100	
fax	+385 (0)52 451 440	
email	reservations-porec@valamar.com	
web	www.valamar.com	

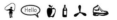

Map 1 Entry 10

Residence Parentino

Obala Maršala Tita 15, Poreč, 52440 Istria

An Austrian entrepreneur began the hotel business in Opatija. Unable to obtain a construction permit for Poreč, then the political centre of Istria, he settled instead for a portion of the sea in the town's harbour – purchased from insurance brokers Lloyd's. He then filled in his patch of water and created the Pore Riviera, one of the defining landmarks of the city today. The Parentino was the first of his hotel ventures (Jadran, Isabella and Neptun are others): an early 20th-century seaside residence with elegant bedrooms that face the seafront, and a restaurant that serves fish from the bay and the crisp white wines of Istria's rich red soils. The hotel is a bold building, all arches and balustrades, while inside, rooms showcase the standard pure white walls, uncluttered styling and brilliant sea views of the Riviera hotels. For a watery escape, visit the gorgeous swimming pool of partner hotel Fortuna just along the coast. Jaunts inland will reveal Istria's inspiring interior of rolling countryside, vineyards and fortified hilltop towns. *Minimum stay three nights.*

rooms	14 doubles.
price	€36–€92. Singles €24–€57. Buffet half-board extra €6 p.p.
meals	Lunch & dinner, à la carte, from €75 for 2.
closed	November–April.
directions	On Poreč promenade. Detailed directions on booking.

Hotel

Reservations	
tel	+385 (0)52 465 100
fax	+385 (0)52 451 440
email	reservations-porec@valamar.com
web	www.valamar.com

Map 1 Entry 11

Fiorentino

Kovači 17, Kaštelir, 52464 Istria

The modern world may be catching up with Istria, but this is a throwback to an earlier age. Squeezed into the buildings of an old distillery in the sprawling, wine-making village of Kaštelir-Labinci is this appealing country-style apartment for guests and a wonderfully atmospheric bar and living room in the distillery itself. Pull up a bar stool and try the homemade, herb-infused liqueurs (and marmalades) prepared by the family who have owned this land for 150 years. Along with son Karlo, who speaks good English, Ljiljana Grebac runs the place like a family home. The guest apartment's old stone walls contain antique country furniture and folksy arts and crafts – a wall cross here, a wooden hat stand there – and you sleep on delightful Istrian beds with carved wooden headboards. There's a kitchen, a bathroom and your own little garden, with barbecue and sun terrace. The family know the area inside out and will tell you all about the cobblestone villages and the rolling hills around Kaštelir-Labinci. Village walks, wine tours and trips to the sea are the highlights here.

rooms	Apartment for 4.
price	€45-€70.
meals	Self-catering. Restaurant 200m.
closed	October-April.
directions	From Poreč, signed road straight to Kaštelir, 8km. Detailed directions on booking.

	Karlo Grebac
tel	+385 (0)52 455 312
mobile	+385 (0)98 936 2435
email	ljiljana.grebac@pu.htnet.hr

Self-catering

Map 1 Entry 12

Villa Moncitta

Mocitada 69, Karojba, 52423 Istria

In the valley below Višnjan, the villa sits in deep, green seclusion. Designed with the needs of the Fox family in mind, the interiors are generous and sweeping, the walls and floorboards decked in warm creams and ethereal whites. Local craftsmen used traditional stone, pine and oak to create delightfully contemporary spaces – and open fireplaces transform the house into the snuggest winter bolthole. Croatia-born Gordana met Roger when they were young; now they live in London and run the house as a holiday retreat. There are two parts and you may rent either: the main house with its kitchen, dining room, two bathrooms and five bedrooms, or the two-bedroomed side wing. Outside, by the large, languorous pool, is a wonderful summer house with shower, summer kitchen and grill. Hard to leave when you have grapes, figs and walnuts to pluck from the grounds and a cool loggia to retreat to, its upper tier promising glorious views. The hilltops of Motovun and Višnjan are nearby, as are the truffle-rich forests, the sea is a 20-minute drive and the local restaurants are splendid.

Self-catering

rooms	House for 10. Wing for 4.
price	House £900-£1,900. Wing £500-£1,000. Whole place £1,200-£2,750. Prices per week.
meals	Self-catering. Restaurants 5km.
closed	Never.
directions	From Pazin, 18km northwest to Karojb; 3km west to Višnjan; continue north 2km.

Gordana & Roger Fox

tel	+44 (0)20 8883 3771
mobile	+44 (0)7930 550 168
fax	+44 (0)20 8444 6782
email	goga@croatia-villas.com
web	www.croatia-villas.com

Map 1 Entry 13

Rubble Hovel

12 Rocky Road, Pebbleness, Stony Broke, 80000 Istria

Stone shelters are two a penny. And every country gives them a different name. In Istria they are kažun, in Italy they are *casitas*, on Malta they are *girna*, in Ireland *clochan*, in Germany *weinbergshäuschen*… we could go on. All are crudely the same, a collection of stones providing shelter for shepherds and peasant folk. On balmy evenings, you can hear the haunting lilt of pipes from the low rocky huts on the hillsides of Istria. What an experience to stay! A chance to dash back through the centuries and bed down on crude blankets with an oil lamp for light and a pitcher for water. Who needs air conditioning when thick stones keep interiors cool and peaceful? And then there's the perk of sleeping in a national icon. Kažuns vary from valley to valley. Some are round turrets, others square blocks topped by tiled stone roofs; the best have chimneys for a fire. Finding a kažun is simply a case of looking – the hillsides are littered with them, no need to book. Just don't be surprised if a shepherd decides to pitch up for the night. *No air conditioning.*

rooms	Varies. Roof optional.
price	Ideal for skinflints.
meals	Rock candy available.
closed	Always open…
directions	From somewhere, 400km nowhere. Detailed directions not available.

Hovel

	Mr Barn E Rubble
tel	none
email	rubble@pebbles.rocks
web	www.rubble.rocks

Map 1 Entry 14

Špinovci

Špinovci 88, Karojba, 52423 Istria

Reached through rolling countryside outside Motovun, Špinovci is the domain of the jolly Tikel family, who've tended these lands for 300 years. In the cradle of a valley, ringed by fields, forests and isolated farmhouses, Špinovci casts its gaze over a rural dream of olive groves and vineyards, with the peak of Motovun in the background. Older generations of the family recall the tiny wine train that used to pass through, gathering grapes and olives. The track is now a way for hikers, cyclists and groups of horseriders, who trot the path to Trieste. The apartments, traditional, tidy and with kitchenettes, are thoroughly in touch with their surroundings. The crow of cockerels and the hee-haw of donkeys is your morning alarm call; farm cows and chickens provide your milk and eggs. Home-cooked breakfast and supper is served in the family restaurant overlooking the valley – start the day with Istrian ham, finish with succulent wild boar and village wines. Immerse yourself in the good life: join the hunt for truffles, forage for wild asparagus and mushrooms, collect chestnuts to toast in the open fire. *Bikes available for hire.*

rooms	3 apartments: 1 for 4, 2 for 2.
price	280 Kn-320 Kn.
meals	Supper 100 Kn-130 Kn.
closed	January.
directions	Directions on booking.

Restaurant with rooms

	Denis Tikel
tel	+385 (0)52 683 404
fax	+385 (0)52 683 404
email	mario.tikel@pu.htnet.hr

Map 1 Entry 15

Ravnica Cultural Centre

Ravnica 8, Livade, 52427 Istria

An enclave of culture in a deep country setting. Ravnica is a poetic place that perches alone on a ledge in the misty, majestic Mirna valley. Up a dirt track, a mile from the truffle town of Livade, the Radovanovićs' home has become a Centre for Cultural Exchange; during Motovun's famous film festival in July, the house doubles up as an art gallery. Alison was a curator who moved from the UK with Balkan-born husband Rajko; both are lovers of the arts. Ravnica, still a work in progress, was a ruin when they arrived; now each space is energised by a piece of conceptual art. It is a huge-scale undertaking and this energetic couple are actively involved; it is they who man-handled timbers and stones and painted the shutters a fetching Cyan blue. The studio apartment is to one side, its oak beams and terracotta flagstones typical of mid-19th-century architecture. Alison and Rajko may invite you to share supper – both love to cook – and discuss art and philosophy before a rustic open fire. You will be spellbound by the valley views.

rooms	Apartment for 2.
price	300 Kn.
meals	Self-catering. Dinner 50 Kn-100 Kn, by arrangment.
closed	Never.
directions	From Motovun, 3km north to Livade. Right at central Livade roundabout, 500m eastwards; left up road, then track signed Ravnica to end, 500m.

	Alison & Rajko Radovanović
tel	+385 (0)52 664 026
mobile	+385 (0)98 788 867
email	info@ravnica.org
web	www.ravnica.org

Self-catering

Map 1 Entry 16

Bella Vista
Gradiziol 1, Motovun, 52424 Istria

Balanced, eyrie-like, on an Istrian hilltop, Motovun is arguably the prettiest town in the region. UNESCO-listed, its cobbled streets are mostly closed to traffic – no doubt to the chagrin of its most famous son, racing driver Mario Andretti. The countryside is no less inviting: hills cloaked in vines and dense woodland guarding Istrian truffles. This old stone townhouse could provide the backdrop for the balcony scene in *Romeo and Juliet*, while inside are two apartments: one big, one compact, both served by heart-stopping views from the balconies. Interiors are modern and pristine; bunches of dried wild flowers and chunky stone around the windows create a pleasing country mood. The place is run with good-natured efficiency by Mirjana Kotiga, a vivacious Motovun woman who enjoys inviting guests in for coffee at her house in town. She may even take you truffle-hunting in the hills with her keen-nosed hound. As well as being a gastronomic haven, its streets dotted with restaurants and delis, Motovun hosts a film festival in July, pulling in 20,000 film buffs from all over Europe.

rooms	2 apartments for 2-4.
price	€50-€100.
meals	Self-catering. Restaurants, winery & market nearby.
closed	Never.
directions	From Pula south towards Pazin, 22km. From Pazin road to Karojba, 20 mins. Right for Motovun, to centre. Guests only to top of hill. 50m before, opposite shop 'Eva'. Signed.

Self-catering

	Mirjana Kotiga
tel	+385 (0)52 681 724
mobile	+385 (0)91 523 0321
fax	+385 (0)52 681 724
email	info@apartmani-motovun.com
web	www.apartmani-motovun.com

Map 1 Entry 17

Hotel Kaštel
Trg Andrea Antico 7, Motovun, 52424 Istria

Perched on its conical hill is glorious Motovun. Its streets are lined with
Venetian-style mansions, its buildings are girdled by robust medieval walls,
and all around lies dense woodland where gastronomes hunt for truffles and
wild asparagus. Kaštel stands at the highest point on the ridge, tucked in beside
the vaguely Florentine church of Sv Stefano. On arrival, guests are met at the
bottom of the town and ferried up through steep cobbled alleyways to the top.
Kaštel, Motovun's only hotel, has the town's finest site. The Eric family took it
on eight years ago and promptly gave it a smart modern makeover. Winding stone
passageways open into rooms with interesting angles, coordinated furnishings and
modern touches. This is an old building so the bedrooms vary in flavour and size;
our favourite flourishes a balcony with a baron's view over village and valley. The
hotel has two restaurants, one serving modern pasta dishes infused with truffles;
in summer, breakfast is taken alfresco, in a sun-dappled courtyard shaded by
ancient chestnut and mulberry trees.

rooms	30: 15 doubles, 3 singles, 10 triples, 2 suites.	
price	€67–€113. Single €39–€55.50. Triple €92.50–€115.50. Suite €124.50–€151.50. Half-board extra €5 p.p. Full-board extra €10 p.p.	
meals	Breakfast €6. Dinner €10.	
closed	Never.	
directions	Up hill to pedestrianised old town. Hotel on left of town square.	

	The Eric family	Hotel
tel	+385 (0)52 681 607	
fax	+385 (0)52 681 652	
email	info@hotel-kastel-motovun.hr	
web	www.hotel-kastel-motovun.hr	

Map 1 Entry 18

Motovun Ranch

Brkač, Motovun, 52424 Istria

Just beyond Motovun, in the natural bowl of a valley surrounded by lush, green hills, lies Renata and Ivo Vrtarić's ranch. These undisturbed pastures go on for as far as the eye can see. This is also the home of six handsome horses, the main draw for the various youth groups that settle into the dormitory next to the paddock. Ivo and Renata moved to Motovun to escape the bustle of the noisy Croatian capital. Ivo still lectures at Zagreb's Academy of Fine Arts – his equestrian short film *Red Cavalry* premiered at the Motovun Film Festival in 2005. Art installations are an integral part of life back at the Ranch, its table and fireplace fully functioning artistic expressions. Adorning the house are giant modernist metal and iron sculptures, while an intriguing white creation dangles from the mulberry tree outside. Guests have use of a sprawling space occupying three floors: charmingly simple bedrooms at the top, living room with fireplace in the middle, kitchen/dining below. The ranch feels superbly remote; your only immediate neighbours have a craving for sugar lumps and handfuls of wild grass.

Ranch & self-catering

rooms	3: 1 triple; 1 twin, 1 quadruple sharing shower. Dormitory available. Guest kitchen.
price	€40. Whole house €160.
meals	Self-catering. Restaurants 5km.
closed	November-February.
directions	From Motovun, 3km; ranch signed. Call for directions if needed.

Ivo Vrtarić

tel	+385 (0)52 681 798
mobile	+385 (0)98 411 404
email	motovun-ranch@mail.inet.hr
web	www.motovun-ranch.com

Map 1 Entry 19

Agroturizam Matijašić
Pekasi, Motovun, 52424 Istria

Crowning a hill in the heart of Istria's wine country, close to Motovun, the manor has been the family seat of the Matijašićs for 400 years. Its rugged stone walls and exposed dark wood beams speak of another age, when Istria was untouched by the modern world. Little seems to have changed: the floorboards still utter a satisfying creak as you step over the threshold, and the surrounding countryside is pure rural Istria. The old-world feel continues in the cottage: furniture is of the thick, sturdy variety; beds are topped with starched white sheets. Darko Matijašić ushers you into his family home, a welcoming glass of wine in hand. Viticulture has been the family's trade for centuries and they still produce some of the finest vintages in Istria. The family prepare delectable meals from organic, home-grown produce, too, and have a *konoba* nearby. From the grounds, arresting views lie on all sides. The dense surrounding forests are home to wild boars, roe deer, pheasants and rabbits – a superb hunting spot in the days when this area formed the border between the Austrian and Venetian empires.

rooms	1 cottage for 6.
price	900 Kn.
meals	Self-catering. Restaurant 5km.
closed	Never.
directions	From Motovun, 2km to Buje-Buzet road; 3km northwest; towards Butoniga lake, 4km; right to Zamaski dol village.

	Darko Matijašić	Self-catering
tel	+385 (0)52 682 126	
fax	+385 (0)52 682 012	
email	darko.matijasic@pu.t-com.hr	
web	www.matijasic.hr	

Map 1 Entry 20

House Ivela

Pariži 109a, Pazin, 52000 Istria

In the hands of painter and interior designer Ivo Paris, this quaint little village farmhouse has become a work of art. A single glance takes you from aged wood to fabrics in primary colours and exposed stonework framed by pastel-coloured plaster. The 350-year-old ruin has even appeared in *Elle Deco*, its renovation blending traditional features (exposed beams, wooden floors) with creative inspiration and imaginative colours. The atmosphere is more artist's studio than holiday home – Ivo's paintings light up the walls and the main impression is one of space, light and colour. The house is surrounded by woodland and fields of lavender and Ivo and Marija, who live next door, are passionate about all things natural, growing their own vegetables and collecting herbs from the meadows. Happy to engage with guests, they can arrange herbalism and painting courses if you are keen. Colours are eye-catching, bold but never overpowering, and the bathroom has a semi-sunken bathtub to sink into. Ask nicely and Ivo may give you some lavender oil to aid your soaking. *Minimum stay five nights.*

Self-catering

rooms	House for 4.
price	€49–€79 per night. 20% reduction if fewer than 3 people.
meals	Self-catering. Restaurants 3km.
closed	January–March.
directions	From Pazin, 11km on Stara Cesta toward Žminj, then right for Pariži (1km). Detailed directions on booking.

	Ivan Paris
tel	+385 (0)52 686 271
mobile	+385 (0)98 638 813
email	house_ivela@yahoo.com
web	houseivela.netfirms.com

Map 1 Entry 21

Agroturizam Ograde
Lindarski katun 60, Pazin, 52000 Istria

Agrotourism is not a new concept in Istria and the Šajina family have spearheaded the movement – to bring an authentic experience of farm life to visitors who seek more than a sun tan. Set in richly cultivated countryside, Ograde is a working farm busy with horses, cows, sheep, dogs, cats, domestic fowl – and a quartet of peacocks to provide a surreal dawn chorus each morning. Immerse yourself in it all. You might find yourself corralling sheep in the fields or grooming the gorgeous farm horses – it's hands-on here. The stone and timber farmhouses are built in an earthy village style, the interiors are crammed with locally crafted furniture and ornaments, and the bed coverings were woven in Žminj. Choose rooms in the annexe of the bustling family home, or rent the one-storey cottage in the grounds. Meals are a family affair and the menus work their way around the ingredients available on any given day. As well as gaining experience of farming life, you can stroll or ride horses in the pristine countryside, and learn how to cook Istrian-style in the huge country kitchen.

rooms	Apartment for 6. Cottage for 6.
price	Apartment €60–€110. Cottage €60-€120.
meals	Self-catering. Breakfast €5. Lunch & dinner around €15.
closed	Never.
directions	From Pula, Poreč, Rovinj & Vrsar take 'Istrian Y' road; exit Žminj; cont. to centre; take road on right to Pazin. On exiting Žminj, follow sign for Lindarski katun on right.

Self-catering

	Davorka Šajina
tel	+385 (0)52 693 035
mobile	+385 (0)98 723 442
fax	+385 (0)52 616 461
email	agroturizam-ograde@pu.t-com.hr
web	www.agroturizam-ograde.hr

Map 1 Entry 22

Leader

Lupoglav 8, 52426 Istria

Combining 'heritage' with 'modern' requires subtlety. Some places go too far and stray into Disneyland territory; this resort stays the right side of the line. At first glance, the six conical cottages in the hills appear to be modest in the extreme. Do not be misled! Behind the rustic stone walls hide delicious creature comforts – hot showers, air conditioning, central heating and glowing wood fires. Owner Ivan Baričević designed the dwellings in sympathy with the kažun (shepherds' shelters) strewn on the hillsides across Istria – but no shepherd ever had life as easy as this! The cottages sit in tree-shaded grounds behind a country-style restaurant that serves good mountain food – venison, wild boar, truffles, all from the hills. It's a superb set-up for families, with its pool, tennis courts, riding school and pen full of rabbits. Healthy outdoor activities are followed by big suppers... and early nights. This is a gentle resort in a modest village (just a handful of shops and tavernas); ask Ivan about pony rides to the peak of Mount Planik, and views that stretch to the Alps. *Bikes available for hire.*

Resort

rooms	6 cottages for 2.
price	280 Kn-400 Kn.
meals	Breakfast 25 Kn. Lunch & dinner 70 Kn-150 Kn.
closed	Never.
directions	From Buzet, 17km southeast, to Lupoglav. Detailed directions on booking.

Ivan Baričević

tel	+385 (0)52 685 300
fax	+385 (0)52 685 251
email	josip.baricevic@pu.t-com.hr
web	www.istraleader.com

Map 1 Entry 23

Boško Apartments

A. Motovunjanina 14, Rovinj, 55210 Istria

Boško and his wife Dragana are passionate about kiwi fruit – their exotic vines coil over the canopies that extend from the garden gate to the door. Close to sandy beaches on the islet-studded coast near Rovinj, this modern house is nothing exceptional but has been brought to life by its charmingly eccentric owners. Don't be surprised if you open the door to a large rabbit lolloping in the hall. The ebullient Boško loves to regale guests with tales of local derring-do; this couple have a deep knowledge of the town and the area so make the most of them. Their neat and tidy home is enhanced by unexpected angles and sunlight flooding in. Furnishings are modern and functional, the décor enlivened by patches of primary colour. Studios and apartments are completely self-contained – bedrooms, bathrooms, living rooms, kitchenettes – and the gardens beautifully tended, as you might expect. It's a short drive to the old town of Rovinj, its perfect cliff-fringed islands and its statuesque Church of Sv Eufemija. The beaches of Istria's sand-dusted 'golden coast' lie not much further.

rooms	4 studios for 3-4. 6 apartments for 2-6.
price	Studios €25–€59. Apartments €46–€98.
meals	Self-catering. Restaurants within 150m.
closed	Never.
directions	Just outside Rovinj town centre, follow road to Bale. Detailed directions on booking.

Self-catering

	Boško & Dragana Kovačević
tel	+385 (0)52 830 329
mobile	+385 (0)98 560 846
fax	+385 (0)52 830 329
email	bosko.kovacevic@pu.htnet.hr
web	www.bos-ko.com

Map 1 Entry 24

Mofardin Agroturizam

Veštar 4, Rovinj, 52210 Istria

A vision of Istria as it must once have been, this aeons-old stone farmhouse, at the end of a dusty track, has the motto '*Nema Stressa*' ('no stress') inscribed above the bar. You are unlikely to feel anything other than soothed by these rustic surroundings. It's a wonderfully wholesome place, overseen by Roberto and his mother Luisa: long, heart-warming suppers of roast suckling pig and home-grown wine, followed by homemade sheep's cheese, polished off with a thimbleful of herb-infused grappa. Bedrooms are cosy throwbacks to another age: beams line the ceilings and furniture has been passed down the family, from the dark wooden dressers to the horse cart in the grounds. Bed down in the roomy old house, or take a smart room in the more private but less characterful new building. The farmland is yours to discover – cats and dogs wander the grounds, hens and pheasants peck in the undergrowth – and the setting is a nature lover's joy, wild Brijuni deer passing by on their way from one wooded copse to another. The sea is a step away: pine and oak trees stand like sentinels guarding its shores.

rooms	6 doubles.
price	€45–€62.
meals	Lunch & dinner €8–€20.
closed	October–March.
directions	From Rovinj, 5km southeast on the road to Bale; turn right & continue 1km towards Veštar. Detailed directions on booking.

Guest house

	Roberto Mofardin
tel	+385 (0)52 829 044
fax	+385 (0)52 829 044
email	roberto.mofardin@pu.htnet.hr

Map 1 Entry 25

Villa Valdibora

Silvana Chiurca 8, Rovinj, 52210 Istria

Aristocratic Valdibora squeezes itself between medieval mansions in the very heart of Rovinj's Old Town. The listed townhouse was built in the 1700s and still feels like a throwback to the era of Franco-Venetian rule, with its grand library taking up most of the ground floor, and its portrait of Napoleon's mistress hanging in the entrance hall (he once lived next door). Private rooms and communal spaces, dotted with oil paintings and antiques, have been styled with stately finesse. Yet the mood is delightfully intimate. Expect sloping ceilings, gracious dining tables and chairs on old stone floors, delicate wrought-iron bedsteads, saunas, state-of-the-art bathrooms, comfortable sofabeds in living rooms and even laptops to hire – a perfect marriage of period splendour and modern-day comfort. Staff serve you breakfast, clean your apartments daily, take care of your laundry and lend you the villa's bikes so you may explore the winding cobblestone streets and imagine youself back in the days when Venetian merchant ships lined the bustling harbour.

rooms	4 apartments for 2-4.
price	€110–€200 for two. Discounts for children.
meals	Self-catering. Breakfast included. Restaurants 1km.
closed	Never.
directions	In Rovinj Old Town, 50m from harbour. Detailed directions on booking.

Self-catering

	Ivana Botica
tel	+385 (0)52 845 040
fax	+385 (0)52 845 050
email	valdibora@email.com
web	www.valdibora.com

Map 1 Entry 26

Apartments Venema

Augusto Ferry 35, Rovinj, 52210 Istria

Tucked down a maze of alleys in Rovinj Old Town, surrounded by townhouses painted jewel-like colours, the Apartments Venema crouch under the protective wing of Sv Eufemija. All around you: a sea of shuttered windows and gently pitched roofs, rising to the baroque church spire that has stood above the rooftops of Rovinj like a beacon for three centuries, guiding sailors home. The colours of Venema reflect those of the Old Town: summery yellows and autumnal oranges. A modern construction in Dalmatian style, the house is split into two self-catering apartments. Low attic ceilings create an intimate feel upstairs, while the rooms on the lower floor are newer in feel and less atmospheric. The setting is the thing, in the old town but with views of the bay and minutes from the beach. In summer, the streets are enlivened by outdoor art, green parks and promenades. Close offshore is an unusual attraction – the century-old wreck of the *Baron Gautsch*, one of Croatia's most popular diving sites.

rooms	2 apartments for 2-4.
price	400 Kn–600 Kn.
meals	Self-catering. Restaurants within 50m.
closed	Never.
directions	From Rovinj seafront, northwards. Detailed directions on booking.

Self-catering

	Željko Pitić
tel	+385 (0)1 369 8332
mobile	+385 (0)98 218 904
fax	+385 (0)1 369 8330
email	venema@vip.hr
web	www.apartmani-rovinj.com

Map 1 Entry 27

Stancija Meneghetti
Bale, 52211 Istria

Ten hectares of olive groves, vineyards and meadows are the backdrop to this remote Istrian villa. The mood is one of quiet country luxury, so come to relax and enjoy fine food and privacy. The 100-year-old farmhouse has been modernised in sympathy with its surroundings. Sumptuous rooms have elegant furniture, shuttered windows, glass walls and skylights to draw in the light. Exposed beams curve overhead like ships' timbers, adding to the classical mood. The main bedroom is fabulous – a vast, brick-lined space warmed by an open fire in winter, its big bathroom with vineyard views; gaze on them as you soak. There are indoor and outdoor swimming pools to dive into, truffle-hunting books in the library to browse, a fire for toasting your toes, a sauna to luxuriate in. All has been designed with families in mind: a glass wall looks onto both the indoor pool and the walled lawns in front of the terrace. And you have a caretaker, a housekeeper and two gifted chefs (just pay for the ingredients). At the attached winery, taste wines straight from the cellar, or order from a sophisticated list of labels. *Bikes available for hire.*

rooms	Villa for 10.
price	€750–€900.
meals	Breakfast included. Catered or self-catering.
closed	Never.
directions	From Bale, take turning to camp Colone, next to football field; after 5km, left at sign for Meneghetti. Follow road for 2km to Stancija Meneghetti estate.

Catered villa & self-catering

	Davorin Skoko
mobile	+385 (0)91 2431 600
fax	+385 (0)1 242 2815
email	info@meneghetti.info
web	www.meneghetti.info

Map 1 Entry 28

Eia Eco Art Village

San Zuian 13, Bale, 52211 Istria

Eia Eco Art Village had been a boyhood dream for Igor. After travelling –
footloose in Africa and Asia, then working as a holistic therapist in London – he
returned to Istria to resurrect his great-grandfather's wilderness retreat. In a
Sixties-style vision of utopia, alternative-minded travellers are at one with nature;
two uninhabited hectares yours to roam, and your bedroom a strawbale house or
tent. Water comes from harvested rain and there are some modest modern
conveniences like rudimentary showers and a well-equipped kitchen in Igor's
environmentally designed house. Field systems flow, donkeys bray, cats bask, sheep
flock, chickens potter and pacifists strum. It's a communal style of living that will
hit a sweet note with the right kind of traveller. As part of a stay, you may join a
course in photography, permaculture, meditation and shamanic dance. Or just
help out on the land. Luxury of luxuries: there's an Indian sweat lodge, a
precursor of the sauna. Igor is a generous man, living at one with nature,
delighted to share his vision of a perfect world.

Camp

rooms	Strawbale house for up to 12. Caravan for 4-5. Shared kitchen & showers. Camping possible.
price	€5 p.p.
meals	Self-catering.
closed	Never.
directions	3km from Bale dir. Krmed. From Rijeka or Kopar on Y road, exit Rovinj. After 4km, right for Pula/Bale. After 6km, left for Krmed; 300m after crossing, right at sign for Eia; 300m gravel track.

	Igor Drandić
mobile	+385 (0)98 916 0650
email	eia@pu.htnet.hr
web	www.eia.hr

Map 1 Entry 29

Porer Lighthouse
Porer Island, Istria

Hard to imagine a more remote setting than this. Porer Lighthouse, a lonely spur of masonry, stands on a low, treeless islet measuring 80m from side to side. This the lighthouse of Enid Blyton adventure stories, a tower on a rocky skerry surrounded by crashing waves. Who would guess it were 30 minutes from Istria's tip? Although the isle is rocky (don't expect beaches) the surrounding waters teem with fish, and snorkellers and divers may even spot the odd shipwreck exposed on the sandy sea bed. Constructed in 1833, it is one of the oldest surviving lighthouses on the Adriatic. The lighthouse keepers get to stay in the tower while guests have two separate apartments below, simple but comfortable, perfect for seekers of solitude. As Porer is so tiny and arid, trips to Pula, the bays of Unije Island and the islet of Fenoliga (where dinosaur tracks may be detected) can be fixed with the ferryman, Captain Ivan Giotta. Stock up on provisions and lose yourself in books, fishing, art. The sunsets are said to be the most beautiful in the Adriatic. *Minimum stay seven nights in summer. No heating.*

rooms	2 apartments for 4.
price	€499–€799 per week.
meals	Self-catering. Provisions available at extra charge.
closed	Never.
directions	Take Pula bypass (12km); follow signs for Premantura & Pomer. Boat from Premantura (30 mins/€100). Mornings only. Arrange in advance.

Lighthouse

	Adriatica.net
tel	+44 (0)20 7183 0437
fax	+385 (0)1 245 2909
email	info@adriatica.net
web	www.adriatica.net

Map 1 Entry 30

Villa Primorka

Veli Brijuni, Brijuni Islands, 52214 Istria

For over a century, the Brijuni islands have been fêted by artists and writers, politicians and royals. More recently, Tito used it as his summer playground, hosting visiting celebrities at the islands' luxurious villas. (Elizabeth Taylor, Jaqueline Kennedy and Josephine Baker were all guests; Sophia Loren was his favourite.) Positioned on Lovorika Bay on the southeastern shore of Veli Brijuni, this extraordinary villa creates the impression of utter privacy, blessed as it is with lush gardens and a private beach. And yet you are a 15-minute walk from the port. To stay here is to experience the glamour of the 1950s; furnishings are original, fabulously retro; rooms are grand and capacious, with warm parquet floors and rugs that run for ever. Arrive by private yacht, or be collected by theirs. A housekeeper is present – discreetly; a chef and a waiter can be hired. How charming to be served freshly-caught seafood at the villa's gracious dining table – or out on the sea-facing terrace. Don't expect cutting-edge luxury, this is style of an older, grander kind. *Minimum stay three nights.*

Catered villa

rooms	Villa for 8.
price	€1,030–€1,350 per night.
meals	Catering extra charge. Meals can be delivered from sister hotel. Restaurants in Veli Brijuni.
closed	December–January.
directions	Airport road to Pula; 7km to Fažana; private transfer by boat (15 mins).

	Brijuni National Park
tel	+385 (0)52 525 807
fax	+385 (0)52 521 367
email	brijuni@brijuni.hr
web	www.brijuni.hr

Map 1 Entry 31

Hotel Scaletta

Flavijevska 26, Pula, 52100 Istria

Near the centre of thronging Pula and close to the superb Roman amphitheatre, Scaletta glows with familial warmth. It is all a small, renovated Mediterranean townhouse hotel should be. A dusky-pink façade conceals an uplifting interior: buttercup-yellow and sky-blue walls meet blond wood floors, while dried flower and ribbon arrangements add cosiness. Five members of the German-Croatian Talić family are here to look after guests and do so with an easy charm. Bedrooms are warm, smart, spotless. Bathrooms have a seaside feel, with starfish floors and shell-stencilled borders… and corner baths with rubber ducks! Windows are framed with white shutters. In the main building is an Austro-Hungarian styled restaurant serving international food with an Italian twist. A second restaurant, across the street, is known for its seafood and its roof that retracts on summer nights. For an Italian-style espresso hit, stroll around the corner to Uliks, a coffee shop housed in the building where James Joyce once lived.

rooms	12: 10 doubles, 2 singles.
price	€70–€100. Singles €55–€70.
meals	Lunch & dinner from €10.
closed	Never.
directions	150m north of Pula's amphitheatre, on right. Detailed directions on booking.

	Kristina Talić
tel	+385 (0)52 541 599
fax	+385 (0)52 540 285
email	krtalic@pu.t-com.hr
web	www.hotel-scaletta.com

Hotel

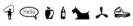

Map 1 Entry 32

Villa Vanda Apartments
Pješčana Uvala VI/28, Pula, 52100 Istria

As increasing numbers wend their way to Pula, those in the know escape to
the suburbs – and avoid tourist bustle. Villa Vanda is a hop and a skip from the
warm waters of the Adriatic, on a prim street in the Pješčana Uvala district,
a playground of marinas, uncrowded sands and pebbled coves. From its balconies,
views sweep to an ocean of intense blue, where small sailing boats pick their way
between forested islands and promontories. These tidy, contemporary apartments
each have a colour scheme: bedspreads, upholstery, bath tiles and towels match.
The best are the red and white apartments with sea views; others are less grand,
yet summery pictures and ornaments in all reflect Mirjana's warm character. She
is open hearted and will gladly chat away, but knows when to give you space too.
If you tire of the beach, the breathtaking relics of Pula are close by, along with
several elegant places that show off Istria's cosmopolitan cuisine – gnocchi with
truffles from Italy, Middle Eastern style herb-filled ćevapčići (mini kebabs), and
local pršut (proscuttio). *Minimum stay three nights.*

rooms	5 apartments for 2-4.
price	€40–€80 per night.
meals	Self-catering. Restaurants 100m.
closed	Never.
directions	Just outside Pula, on road to Vodnjan. Detailed directions on booking.

Self-catering

Mirjana Vanda

tel	+385 (0)52 397 121
mobile	+385 (0)98 506 798
email	info@pjescanauvala.com
web	www.pjescanauvala.com

Map 1 Entry 33

Hotel Valsabbion

Pješčana Uvala IX/26, Pula, 52100 Istria

The first port of call for the fashionistas of the Istrian coast. 'Reception' consists of a desk in the restaurant; the mood here is stylish laid-back. In the Pješčana uvala district of Pula – a playground for yachties – Valsabbion's Deco-effect front hovers above the marina, a vision of contemporary chic. Bedrooms are super-comfortable: beds wear the lushest fabrics, leather sofas nudge tables topped with Zen pieces, shelves carry contemporary objets d'art, smart balconies oversee the marina below. At the top is a wellness centre with hydromassage, infinity pool and every therapy under the sun. This comfortably small boutique hotel is family-run. Sonja Perić takes care of the restaurant and the design while her sister Sandra runs the wellness centre and masterminds the hotel. The restaurant has won awards and the food is fabulous; for ten years now the Valsabbion has been queen of Istrian cuisine. White truffle salad is served on mirrored glass; squid ink risotto arrives on a fragment from an ancient urn. All is seasonal and locally sourced, and the food so good-looking you could wear it.

rooms	10: 6 double, 3 suite, 1 family.
price	€69–€169.
	40% discount for children under 10.
meals	Breakfast €11.50. Lunch €30.
	Dinner €60.
closed	January.
directions	From centre of Pula, 2km southeast to Pješčana uvala. Detailed directions on booking.

	Sonja Perić	Hotel
tel	+385 (0)52 218 033	
fax	+385 (0)52 383 333	
email	info@valsabbion.hr	
web	www.valsabbion.hr	

Map 1 Entry 34

Villa Velike Stine
Regi 44, Medulin, 52203 Istria

Once a sleepy fishing village, Medulin is one of Istria's gems – and one of the few resorts in the area with a sandy beach. Old windmills line the promenade while the remains of Medulin's Roman dwellings have been found in Vizule. This appealing townhouse is set back from the water and conceals a dainty garden, its trim lawns dotted with fruit trees. Fresh white walls lighten what was once a rustic stone house: a Mandalinić family heirloom that Igor, the perfect host, has recently restored and transformed into five tidy, functional, self-catering apartments. Neat rooms have a mix of new and dark wooden family pieces and crisp linens – a signature style for the Istrian coast. Warm evenings are the time to test the efficacy of the stone spit-roast oven in the shared garden – though Igor will cook for you if you ask in advance. The delicacies that come from Medulin's coast are still some of Istria's finest: you can taste black squid ink risotto and fresh crab both here and in the beachside tavernas. *Minimum stay seven days mid-June-mid-September.*

Self-catering

rooms	5 apartments: 3 for 2, 1 for 3, 1 for 4.
price	€30–€70. Half-board extra €13–€25 p.p.
meals	Self-catering. Lunch & dinner about €15. Restaurants 100m.
closed	Never.
directions	Medulin is 7km southeast of Pula. Detailed directions on booking.

Igor Mandalinić

tel	+385 (0)52 394 130
mobile	+385 (0)98 189 2436
email	igor.mandalinic@pu.htnet.hr
web	www.antique.hr

Map 1 Entry 35

Matohanci

Matohanci 16, Kanfanar, 52352 Istria

Run by the kindly Matohanca family, this old-style Istrian house is known for its lovely *konoba* and its Istrian, Italian-touched food based on truffles, pasta and game. Wines are produced by Gloria's father, Nevio, and the vegetables are from the garden. The Matohanci started out as a restaurant, then they added rooms, but the locals still drop by for the food. This is a farmhouse still; the exterior stone walls are dotted with agricultural bric-a-brac dating back to the grandparents' time, while the interiors are country simple. Guests have two large white bedrooms upstairs, with five beds between them – ideal for a family with children. Bathrooms are spotless. Gloria's breakfasts of omelettes stuffed with asparagus, salami and cheese will set you up for a day exploring the Istrian countryside. More active types can choose to go rock climbing at Dvigrad Castle, while gastronomes may go in search of tasty oysters at Lim Fiord. There's a big lawn where children can play – and a friendly dog to fuss over.

rooms	2: 1 doubles, 1 triple.
price	180 Kn-300 Kn.
	Triple 270 Kn-450 Kn.
meals	Lunch & dinner 30 Kn-120 Kn.
closed	Never.
directions	From Rovinj 9km east, then 2km north on Trieste road. On left, 3km before Limski Kanal.

Restaurant with rooms

	Gloria Matohanca
tel	+385 (0)52 848 394
mobile	+385 (0)98 191 0664
fax	+385 (0)52 848 394
email	glorija.matohanca@pu.htnet.hr
web	www.agroistra.com/matohanci

Map 1 Entry 36

Istarska Hiža

Peresiji 15, Svetvinčenat, 52342 Istria

In a tiny Venetian stone village, built by a blacksmith during the Napoleonic era, stands this classic Istrian house. On one side you have the lovely old stone part of the building, topped by terracotta tiles and rustic chimneys. Pass under the cool arch to wooden floors, quaint alcoves and traditional furniture, much of which belonged to Slavko's grandparents; spot them in the faded black and white photographs dotted around. Next door is more modern and split into an apartment and main house. There's less character here, but large rooms and a private terrace amply compensate, and the pretty cobbled front garden is shared. Charming Slavko and his mother-in-law, Zlata, invite guests in as if they were part of the family, preparing tasty dishes from garden vegetables and local game. Wine is from the family vineyard; breakfasts are banquets; meals are lavish – the pasta with truffles is very good. The area is a birdwatchers' paradise, and Slavko can organise sailing trips for the nautically inclined. Nearby is the medieval town of Svetvinčenat, renowned for its annual mime festival.

rooms	2 houses for 4.
price	880 Kn.
meals	Self-catering. Breakfast 40 Kn. Lunch & dinner 75 Kn-120 Kn.
closed	Never.
directions	Exit 'Istrian Y' road at Žminj, then 7.5km south dir. Pula to Svetvinčenat; southeast for 1.5km. Detailed directions on booking.

Self-catering

	Slavko Puh
tel	+385 (0)52 560 446
mobile	+385 (0)98 440 505
fax	+385 (0)52 211 735
email	slavko.puh@pu.t-com.hr

Map 1 Entry 37

Casa Lavignia
Čabrunići 38, Svetvinčenat, 52342 Istria

An old stone house in an old stone village, not far from the gothic splendours of Svetvinčenat. The charming Sanja spent many years in Cornwall before returning to Istria, three teenagers in tow, to resurrect this house. Set in a stony courtyard, backing onto a vast meadow contained by low stone walls, the 100-year-old farmhouse has been beautifully renovated and Sanja's understated interiors owe much to English country design. Rooms are full of character and cared for with love. In the sitting room, crimson walls frame a period fireplace; above is a flame-coloured work of art filling the room with warmth. Upstairs: four bedrooms, with solid wooden beds, brand new mattresses and pale curtains. Bathrooms are chic; in one, citrus walls and a jacuzzi with views. Downstairs is a well-equipped country kitchen; upstairs, a terrace overlooking the old walnut tree in the grassy garden. There's a grocer's in the village – the supermarkets are a bit further – but should your elected chef tire of cooking, Svetvinčenat has some of the best restaurants in the region. *Minimum stay seven nights preferred.*

rooms	House for 8-10.
price	€350 per night.
meals	Self-catering. Restaurants within 7km.
closed	Never.
directions	From Pula, 18km northwards; pass Vodnjan & Juršići; left at sign for Čabrunići. Enter village, cross railtracks & ask for Casa Lavignia.

Self-catering

	Sanja Jović
mobile	+385 (0)91 767 0997
email	sjs_sunshine@hotmail.com
web	www.casalavignia.istra.net

Map 1 Entry 38

House Gabi

Puntera 33, Barban, 52207 Istria

Come for an earthy slice of Istrian village life, in an attractively secluded spot on the outskirts of hilltop Barban. Birds warble in the trees, hens peck in the courtyard, shepherds guide their sheep each morning to the meadows; life moves slowly here. This striking stone cottage goes back 200 years; abandoned in the 1930s, it was restored only two years ago. The owner's daughter, who speaks English, pops in regularly from next door to make sure everyone is happy. Ideal for families, House Gabi resembles an old-fashioned Istrian hunting lodge, with a huge timber balcony overlooking the entrance hall and lots of folksy memorabilia on the walls and window sills. The triple bedrooms are in keeping: homely and rustic with hand-carved antique wooden furniture and exposed stone. To welcome you, the owners prepare a wonderful four-course feast of Istrian dishes, served at gingham-covered tables in the main hall. The setting is remote, the walking is superb and Barban is rich in gothic and baroque architecture – a delight for amateur historians. *Complimentary meal on first night.*

Self-catering

rooms	House for 6.
price	€110–€150.
meals	Self-catering. Restaurants 2km.
closed	Never.
directions	Follow road from Žminj to Barban. On right, just past Barban.

Nika Ružić

tel	+385 (0)52 567 440
mobile	+385 (0)98 166 4850
email	nika.ruzic@public.carnet.hr
web	www.histrica.com/offer/private-accommodation/gabi/

Map 1 Entry 39

Kuća Barmel

Melnica 21, Barban, 52207 Istria

Up a hill, down a vale, around a couple of farms and you arrive at a hamlet surrounded by vineyards. The pink, single storey cottage sits on a small hill just outside Barban and is a quiet country haven. Owners Branko and Vesna are your immediate neighbours – the cottage is an outbuilding on their estate – and they are passionate about looking after guests and making them feel at home. The house is well stocked with local guidebooks which you may attempt to decipher over doughnuts and strong coffee, proffered on arrival by your thoughtful hostess. Bedroom doors open onto cosy yet fresh living spaces furnished with restored country furniture; beds are crafted from twisted olivewood. The vegetable patch is yours to plunder, and the Blažinas will gladly give you some of their own wine and brandy. In spite of their limited English, they do have an uncanny knack of reading your thoughts and knowing your needs. The surrounding fields and forests will entice ramblers and roamers, while Barban is home to a fascinating 'Tilting at the Ring' on horseback event – a centuries-old tradition.

rooms	Cottage for 6 (2 doubles, bunkbeds for 2).
price	€55–€99.
meals	Self-catering. Restaurant in Barban, 1km.
closed	Never.
directions	From Pula, 26km to Barban; 1km to Melnica. Detailed directions on booking.

Self-catering

	Vesna Blažina
tel	+385 (0)52 567 778
fax	+385(0)52 372 114
email	protokol@istra-istria.hr

Map 1 Entry 40

Casa Bianca
Pačići bb, Barban, 52207 Istria

Istria's interior is lovelier even than its coast. It is the Mediterranean as you long for it to be: sleepy, traditional, marked by tiny villages, sprawling vineyards, and meadows bounded by low stone walls. You may not see another foreign tourist for days, but you will get to meet the locals – as yet untouched by tourism. Casa Bianca is every inch the traditional country home – tall stone chimneys, neat wooden shutters, terracotta roofs, an informal terrace for breakfast in the shade and a wine cellar in a converted well topped by aquamarine glass. The owner has added some thoughtful touches to enliven the simple rooms. Find backlit windows in warm colours alongside solid antique beds and wooden dressers, and the odd quirk; the bird's nest in the ceiling was left intact to bring good luck. The villa is well set up for self-caterers, but note that the nearest restaurant is down several meandering lanes. The family greets you on arrival; once settled, you are largely left to your own devices. In a place like this, no bad thing.
Minimum stay one week. Swimming pool planned.

Self-catering

rooms	House for 8.
price	610 Kn-1,320 Kn per week.
meals	Self-catering. Restaurant 2km.
closed	Christmas-mid-January.
directions	From Vodnjan road to Juršići, 4km. Once there, ask at roadside café or bar for Pačići, 4km. The house will be in front of you.

	Mirjana Janko
tel	+385 (0)52 500 418
mobile	+385 (0)91 538 2806
email	mirjana.janko@public.srce.hr

Map 1 Entry 41

Kuća Salvia

Manjadvorci bb, Barban, 52207 Istria

Where the village of Manjadvorci blends into the forest is Kuća Salvia, a tree-sheltered refuge. Named after the medicinal sage that Lorena loves to grow, this cottage has been a "project of passion", each stone set and each tile laid by the Brgić family themselves. The name – Manjadvorci – means 'small castles' but the feel here is of a gypsy haven. Lorena is a chatty, charming landscape painter and her love for this place is evident on the walls – while the exposed stone so typical of Istria's architecture appears in bedroom corners. Guests rent the whole house: two bedrooms plus a kitchen, sitting room, bathroom and garden. The air is heady with the scents of rosemary, sage and blossom, and you overlook sweeping pastures and rising woodland – a treat to explore. Salvija is also handy for the sea, with Raša Bay just six kilometres away. Be sure to sample Lorena's food (cooking is another passion) at some point during your stay, or eat out in medieval, majestic Barban. A comfortable and peaceful place, perfect for art lovers and romantics. *30% supplement for under three nights.*

rooms	Cottage for 5.
price	€50–€100.
meals	Self-catering. Meals available. Restaurant 200m.
closed	Never.
directions	From Pula, 20km northeast to Barban. Detailed directions on booking.

Self-catering

	Lorena Brgić
tel	+385 (0)52 503 834
email	marko.brgic@pu.htnet.hr

Map 1 Entry 42

Stancija Negričani

Stancija Negričani bb, Marčana, 52206 Istria

Beyond historic Vodnjan (famous for its catacombs containing the mummified bodies of local saints), the streets and houses gradually give way to planted fields and wild meadows. Negričani, with its stone chimneys, painted shutters, terracotta tiles and lush woodland, blends in perfectly. The building has been renovated and decorated with flair and each room, including the bathrooms, has a natural theme inspired by the countryside. Bedrooms pamper, while hand-painted details and polished antique pieces add charm. Such rural chic could only have been created by a pair of city eyes: the project was a labour of love for energetic Mirjana Modrušan, who learned the art of hospitality in the bustling restaurants of Pula. With her gentle persuasion, guests are encouraged to chat and interact; this is an unusually friendly hotel. Negričani sprawls across a vast garden that contains a boulder-fringed swimming pool and themed play areas for children. Youngsters will be sure to make friends with resident, nifty-footed tortoises Victoria and David, named after the Beckhams. *Bikes available for hire.*

rooms	7: 2 doubles, 4 twins, 1 family for 4.
price	€60–€105. Family €100–€130.
meals	Breakfast €5–€8. Lunch & dinner from €20.
closed	Never.
directions	From Vodnjan, direction Negričani, left; 6km past Vodnjan, take white unpaved road to Stancija; 300m.

Hotel

Mirjana Modrušan

tel	+385 (0)52 391 084
mobile	+385 (0)91 139 1022
fax	+385 (0)52 580 830
email	konoba-jumbo@pu.t-com.hr
web	www.stancijanegricani.com

Map 1 Entry 43

Apartments Morena & Sabina

Dalmatinska 39, Rakalj, Krnica, 52208 Istria

These pleasing apartments, named after the Valićs' daughters, were first inspired by a steady stream of friends from the city who would pop in at weekends and stay. This early germ of hospitality has bloomed into a small family business, run with just the right balance of professionalism and informality. The house sits proudly at the top of a hill, surrounded by a clipped expanse of lawns that gaze over Raša Bay and its seven lighthouses. Guest rooms are in the annexe, but you will probably use them just for sleeping – Nada and Riko like to treat guests as friends. You will almost certainly be invited to spend time in their house, chatting over Istrian dinners like old friends. Produce comes from the garden's productive vegetable patch and delicacies from local butchers and smallholders. The apartment furniture is a throwback to communist times – unconsciously retro! – while Mrs Valić's needlework adorns every wall. Riko keeps a boat moored down in the bay and often takes guests on fishing adventures among the islands – join him and catch your supper.

rooms	3 apartments: 1 for 6, 2 for 3.
price	€30-€80.
meals	Self-catering.
	Meals €5-€10, by arrangement.
closed	Never.
directions	From Pula take Pula airport road dir. Rijeka (NE); 20km, then right for Krnica and Rakalj; 4km to Krnica; 3km to Rakalj. Through village on Sv Nikola road for 700m.

	Riko Valić	Self-catering
tel	+385 (0)52 556 208	
mobile	+385 (0)98 181 8855	
fax	+385 (0)52 556 373	

Map 1 Entry 44

Apartman Lucija
Antončići 16, Žminj, 52341 Istria

The house is a geranium-covered haven. The scent of roses rises from the porch, barns, haystacks and log piles dot the grounds, and sweet red cherries, ripe plums, tart apples and golden pears drop from the trees. Ondina and her mother welcome guests like long lost relatives and the farm buzzes with animals and activity: eggs are collected, grapes fermented, brandy distilled. A much-loved donkey and goat — firm pals, we're told — munch the lawns, overseen by the occasional garden gnome. Guests are invited to get fully involved with grape picking, goat milking and other farm activities; at night you collapse into a traditional Istrian bed. The apartment has a good kitchen and open-plan living area, but do make the most of Ondina and her husband's cooking; they once worked in a restaurant and cook with the freshest ingredients. Both are charming and speak a smattering of English, while Ondina's mother Lucija communicates through smiles. This is such a heart-warming place that you'll not want to leave — but if you do manage to escape, there's the enchanting hilltop spires of Žminj to explore.

Self-catering

rooms	1 apartment for 4–5.
price	€30–€60.
meals	Self-catering. Breakfast €5. Meals by arrangement. Restaurants 5km.
closed	Never.
directions	From Žminj 3km west on the road to Matijaši. Detailed directions on booking.

Ondina Modrušan
tel	+385 (0)52 825 193
mobile	+385 (0)98 182 2247
fax	+385 (0)52 848 399

Map 1 Entry 45

Obitelj Kuhar
Kuhari 30, Žminj, 52341 Istria

Istria's sprawling hills reveal mountain wineries and medieval towns. If you want to stay in Istria's heart, stay here. Nearby Žminj is the geographical centre of the region, hosts a carnival-like music festival in August – the Bartulja – and has a folk fair every week. Here, a mile down the road, life is lived at a gentler pace. Which is why people love it. Run by the good-natured Ivan and Ruža, Obitelj Kuhar has a pleasingly old-fashioned air. It used to belong to Ivan's father and has its fair share of communist-era furnishings and trims; such décor may have been considered austere 20 years ago but is rather charming today. The couple are great fun and make an effort to be hands-on hosts – you could almost forget the house is self-catering. The kitchen is set up for cooks, but if the appeal of your culinary creations starts to wane, there are a number of restaurants in Žminj. The setting is lovely, on the edge of the village, surrounded by fields and forest; nature almost bursts into the rooms and flowers cascade off balconies and window boxes on every side.

rooms	House for 4.
price	€120.
meals	Self-catering.
	Restaurants in Žminj, 2km.
closed	Never.
directions	From Žminj, 2km. At the petrol pump call owners to collect.

	Ruža Kuhar
tel	+385 (0)52 846 450
mobile	+385 (0)95 900 0550
email	ruza.kuhar@pu.htnet.hr

Self-catering

Map 1 Entry 46

La Casa Di Matiki

Matiki 14, Žminj, 52341 Istria

Sonja Matiki loves to cook, and the smell of cakes and bread just pulled from the oven permeates her vast kitchen. La Casa Di Matiki is a family home, a large, lovely white stone house in a garden filled with animals and trees. Sonja's husband is Italian, and although she grew up in Istria, she has the larger-than-life charm of a much-loved Italian mama. Simple, bright self-catering apartments lie to the back of the building while a separate wing provides newer, larger lodgings. But the big reason to stay is Sonja's cooking and the visitors' book sings her praises. The house is on an old farm on the edge of Žminj and the grounds home to a tribe of friendly animals – dogs, donkeys, horses, chickens, goats. Children would love it here. The comforts are simple, you're in the depths of the countryside, and, unusually for a self-catering place, the family like to get involved with their guests. Breakfasts, lunches and dinners are feasts, served in the kitchen or in the stone courtyard. Another treat is the swimming pool in the grounds – a blessing in the heat of summer. Lie back and drink in the peace.

rooms	5 apartments: 4 for 2-4, 1 for 4-5.
price	€50-€100.
meals	Breakfast €6-€10. Lunch & dinner on request. Restaurant 1km.
closed	Never.
directions	From Rijeka, take 'Istrian Y' road towards Pula. After Pazin, exit left to Žminj, 1km. Turn right at first crossing (petrol station) for Pula. After 1km find sign for Matiki.

Self-catering

	Sonja Glavić-Krivičić
tel	+385 (0)52 846 297
mobile	+385 (0)98 299 040
fax	+385 (0)52 846 297
email	sonja@matiki.com
web	www.matiki.com

Map 1 Entry 47

Agroturizam Ferlin
Gržni 2, Žminj, 52341 Istria

Staying in a tranquil village retreat is one thing; here you engage with rural life. Run by a generous and welcoming family, this old-fashioned farmstay in the countryside near Pazin gives you the chance to do just that. Learn to prepare village meals in the family kitchen at a stone hearth; bend your back in the vineyards beneath a cloudless sky. In this 19th-century home, snug, simple rooms have crisp white linen and country furniture, while bathrooms are small and modestly equipped. On this agroturizam you are introduced to a taste of village life, it is no luxurious escape. Generations of Ferlins have spent their lives here and the farm covers 12 hectares of lavender fields, vineyards, woodland and meadows. It is also home to a tribe of cows, donkeys, chickens, pigs and ducks. All the food brought to the dining table has beens produced on the farm: excellent pršut, bacon, bread, fruit and vegetables. The family is full of smiles, the son is fluent in English and you all eat together in the evenings. Staying on the Ferlin's farm is like visiting family friends. *Minimum stay two nights. Bikes available for hire.*

rooms	4 + 1: 3 doubles, 1 twin. 1 apartment for 4.
price	€15. Apartment €50.
meals	Breakfast €5. Lunch €10. Dinner, 3 courses, €12.
closed	Never.
directions	Road from Barban straight to Žminj. Detailed directions on booking.

	Dinko & Nevenka Ferlin
tel	+385 (0)52 823 515
mobile	+385 (0)98 913 3710
fax	+385 (0)52 823 515
email	neven.ferlin@inet.hr
web	www.histrica.com/offer/agroturizam-ferlin/

Guest house & Self-catering

Map 1 Entry 48

Dea

Šumber 92, Nedešćina, 52231 Istria

Settings don't come much lovelier than this. Mountains rise like a cradle on all sides and eight acres of green and fertile farmland provide a muffler to modern intrusion. Dea, a small cluster of stone and timber dwellings and once part of a noble estate, is a charming place to stay. The enthusiastic Radović family has created four inviting apartments from a former cowshed. Happily, they have resisted the urge to over-modernise: the apartments are endearingly and intimately old-fashioned, with whitewashed walls and low ceilings, raw stonework and homely furnishings. Downstairs is a further, Istrian-style kitchen with a traditional stone oven that warms chilly winter evenings. The family has ambitious plans for the other buildings; for now, their attention is focused on welcoming guests. The eldest son is an experienced guide, happy to share his knowledge of the area – an enticing tapestry of woodland, rolling fields, hamlets, castle ruins, dune-backed beaches and ravines. He is also a stone carver and the faces in the summer kitchen display his talent. *Minimum stay seven nights July/August.*

rooms	4 apartments: 2 for 4, 2 for 4-6.
price	€40–€55 per night.
meals	Self-catering. Breakfast €5.
closed	November-March.
directions	Signed from Labin, 7km; from Rabac, 4km.

Self-catering

	Elide Radović
tel	+385 (0)52 865 599
mobile	+385 (0)91 592 6478
email	elide.radovic@pu.t-com.hr
web	www.radovic-apartments.com

Map 1 Entry 49

Kuća Donada
Ružići 41, Nedešćina, 52232 Istria

On a steep-sided hill in a verdant valley, overlooking fields and forest, Kuća Donada stands alone. The village of Ružići is a scattering of houses and the countryside is peaceful – exceptionally so. Mariza and Josip live and work in Labin and rent out their charmingly renovated holiday house. It may not look special from the outside but step through the door and another world awaits. The attic level has been opened up, suffusing rooms with space and light. Shafts of sunlight spill through the small windows under the eaves; exposed beams throw shadows onto the wooden floors. It is a tasteful and nostalic but un-twee renovation of an Istrian country house. Bedrooms are fuss-free – just a couple of pretty pieces of restored country furniture, a family heirloom here or there, and nicely exposed stonework around the windows. Bathrooms are entirely modern, and a swimming pool is planned, to be set among the neatly groomed lawns. Cultural Labin is ten kilometres away, restaurants are in Sv Martin, and walking is all around.

rooms	House for 9 (3 triples).
price	900 Kn.
meals	Self-catering. Restaurants in Sv Martin, 2km.
closed	Never.
directions	From Labin, 5km west to Marići, then 5.5km north to Sv Martin. Detailed directions on booking.

Self-catering

Mariza Donada

tel	+385 (0)52 858 324
fax	+385 (0)52 856 492
email	mariza.donada@pu.t-com.hr

Map 1 Entry 50

Palača Lazzarini-Battiala

Sv Martin-Kort 33, Nedešćina, 52231 Istria

Exploring the corridors of this atmospheric Venetian home, you almost expect to encounter the ghost of a nobleman. Protected by large grounds, reached via an arcade of 100-year-old chestnut trees, the mansion was built as a summer palace for the enigmatic Count Battiala in 1797. According to legend (and there are plenty) the Battiala family had links to the black-market traders who plied the waters off Labin. The mansion passed to the Lazzarini family by marriage; then, in a fairytale twist of fate, it ended up in the hands of Masimo Jenkel, the grandson of a former servant from the estate. Masimo has a very personal involvement with this lovely place and, along with members of the Belušić and Miletić families, oversaw its restoration from ruin. The three wings have been divided into six eye-catching apartments, rich in classical detail (solid wood furniture, bone china light fittings) and wonderfully peaceful. The president of Croatia, Stjepan Mesić, visited when the place opened and gave it his blessing. Now a swimming pool is being built in the grounds. *Bikes available for hire.*

Self-catering

rooms	6 apartments for 2-5.
price	€45–€67. Singles €30-€35. Heating €10.
meals	Self-catering. Breakfast €5. Dinner €15.
closed	December-March.
directions	Road Labin-Vinež (10km from Labin), 1st crossing on left, turn left to Sv Martin. Through Snašići and Marići to Sv Martin, signed to Palaca.

Dolores Belušić

tel	+385 (0)52 856 006
mobile	+385 (0)91 544 4918
fax	+385 (0)52 880 114
email	info@sv-martin.com
web	www.sv-martin.com

Map 1 Entry 51

Kuća Baronessa
Sv Martin 1, Nedešćina, 52231 Istria

Baronessa is the kind of rural retreat that elderly aunts once visited as part of the Grand Tour. The stone house hides in a verdant valley, 400m above sea level and peaceful as anything. The air is famously stimulating; the village is ringed by forested hills. In the area are little-explored castle ruins, secret beaches and fortified hill towns that exemplify what people love most about Croatia: old Europe as it once was. The story of the house is romantic. It was built for the servants of the noble Lazzarini family but the baron fell in love with one of the staff, transported her to the palace and renamed the staff quarters in her honour. Two years ago the house was converted into a self-catering villa, not extravagant, but ideal for country-loving families. The bedrooms are small and pleasing, and there's room to spread out in the living room, cheery with stone walls, sloping ceiling and comfy black leather chairs. Owner Vladimir is a warm host though his English is limited; his charming ex-wife helps communication flow. She works for a tourist agency in Rijeka – make the most of her!

rooms	House for 6.
price	€86–€120. Pets €7.
meals	Self-catering. Restaurant 2km.
closed	Never.
directions	From Labin 2.5km west towards Sv Martin. Signed off main road.

Self-catering

	Jagoda Cvjetan
tel	+385 (0)51 215 404
mobile	+385 (0)98 726 049
fax	+385 (0)51 215 404
email	vcvjetan@inet.hr

Map 1 Entry 52

Villa Solea

Drenje 29b, Labin, 52220 Istria

Protected by a blanket of wooded hills, Villa Solea overlooks a scattering of islands in a brilliant blue bay. The moment they set eyes on the view Alasdair and Melita knew this was the best possible spot for their new venture. The bold orange chalet-style villa blends traditional stonework with modern detail, including a glass-enclosed winter garden that overlooks the sea and a balcony that gets the sun all day. You can rent the whole house, or take an apartment – there's one up and one down. Upstairs has two bedrooms, downstairs has one plus a sofabed, and interesting details abound – a bright red Miro-esque bedstead here, a curvaceous wrought-iron table there. Bedspreads are dotted prettily with flowers. The simple, elegant dining room seats 15, the breakfast room has windows overlooking the sea on three sides; hard to imagine a finer backdrop to a meal of wind-cured Istrian ham and wild asparagus. The countryside is enchanting; olive trees abound and the oil is rich in flavour. Medieval Labin and the pretty pebble beach at Ravni are an easy drive. *Minimum stay three to seven nights.*

Self-catering

rooms	Villa for 8 (or 2 apartments for 4).
price	Apt for 2-4, £290–£440.
	Apt for 4, £410–£620.
	Whole house £550–£850.
	Prices per week.
meals	Self-catering. Restaurants 2km.
closed	Never.
directions	From Labin, 10km south on road to Ravni. Detailed directions on booking.

	Alasdair & Melita Lacey-Kovac
tel	+44 (0)7776 198 208
fax	+44 (0)7876 821047
email	villasolea@vodafone.net
web	www.villasolea.plus.com

Map 1 Entry 53

Hotel Villa Annette

Raška 24, Rabac, 52221 Istria

An oasis of contemporary calm set against the ancient landscape of Istria's sweeping coast, Hotel Villa Annette has all the hallmarks of the classic boutique hotel. An infinity pool calms the hotel's bustling terrace, shielded by a hundred young olive trees. Overlooking Rabac's lagoon-like bay, the building is the result of the Persić' quest to introduce their own expectations of travel into the design of the hotel. She is an interior designer, her skills endorsed by Croatian president Stjepan Mesić who christened the sprawling Presidential Suite in 2006. A super-comfortable minimalism – cream leatherette armchairs, gleaming modern stone floors – is enlivened by warm colours from beautifully positioned paintings and rugs. And the bedroom suites are huge, with extra sofabeds, countryside views and the islands of Cres and Lošinj in the foreground. Fêted for its cuisine, the hotel is one of the pioneers of the Istrian Slow Food movement. You can even sign up for a Slow Food weekend and discover how to turn the best local ingredients into Croatian-Italian delights.

rooms	12 suites for 2-4.
price	€80–€160. Singles less 20%. Half-board extra €30 p.p.
meals	Lunch & dinner €15–€60.
closed	Never.
directions	From Labin, 5km east to Rabac; signed.

	Vladimir Persić	Hotel
tel	+385 (0)52 884 222	
mobile	+385 (0)98 219 756	
fax	+385 (0)52 884 225	
email	villa.annette@pu.t-com.hr	
web	www.villaannette.hr	

Map 1 Entry 54

Kvarner: the heavenly gateway

This is a place that most people pass through but many miss, in the rush to reach Istria and the Dalmatian coast. A shame: Kvarner's landscape, a mix of straggling islands, seaside resorts, national parks and mountains, is among the most dramatic and diverse in Croatia, a natural playground for fans of the great outdoors.

The mighty Velebit Massif (and National Park) forms a natural border between the coastal plain and the rugged Croatian interior. The atmosphere is tangibly different on the two sides of the ridge, but you find a meeting of minds in the silence of the peaks and the sweet scents of aromatic herbs, pine and sea breezes.

Further south are two more dramatic national parks. Risnjak is the home of bears and rare mountain lynxes, a paradise for wildlife, hiking and adventure sports. Contained within its boundaries are the snowy peaks of Gorski Kotar, centre of the small but growing Croatian ski industry. The other great park here is Plitvice Lakes, a UNESCO-protected string of mountain waterfalls encircled by dense forest.

In the north of Kvarner are the Adriatic islands of Rab, Cres, Krk and Lošinj, less well-known than the islands of Dalmatia but no less beautiful. The human population is concentrated in Rijeka, a bustling port on the mainland and the embarkation point for boats and buses to the west and south of the country. Moving westward around the bay, the pretty seaside towns of Lovran and Opatija bear the neo-gothic hallmarks of the Hapsburgs; watched over by the rugged peaks of Mount Učka, they ruled this coastline for centuries.

Krk, a long, sprawling island connected to the mainland by a toll bridge, is known as 'the golden island' – an allusion to its pebble beaches and rocky 'karst'. Visitors are drawn by nature, sunsets, sunshine and sea, plus the striking medieval town of Krk. Historically, the island was famed for its olive oil, wine and honey; now it is better known for the airport that serves Rijeka. Rab is another tourist resort – the most southerly island of Kvarner, leading down to Dalmatia.

During June the entire island of Cres is strewn with fragrant purple sage blossom. Cres and Lošinj to the south have been inhabited for thousands of years. Many villages were settled in Roman times, while ancient Greek names persist in the hills. The hilltop town of Beli, on Cres, is a popular escape, the domain of rare, protected griffon vultures. On Lošinj, you can see wild dolphins gambolling in the Adriatic surf.

Photo Hotel Kanajt, entry 71

Kvarner

Villa Dubrava
Maršala Tita 188/4, Opatija, 51410 Primorje-Gorski Kotar

Hapsburg emperor Franz Joseph announced the creation of a health resort for the Austro-Hungarian empire in the village of Opatija in 1888. Nobility descended – for the climate and the healing sea air. In its time, it was as fashionable as Nice and Monaco. The grandeur has faded but the healing continues, as part of the pampering Thalassotherapia Opatija complex. A half-century old, the centre promises an amazing range of therapies, some cosmetic, some medicinal. Expect to be slathered in warm mud, pummelled and kneaded with minerals and marinated in essential oils and herbal wraps. Attached by a heated walkway, the Secessionist Villa Dubrava has a gem of a façade, all baroque flourishes, columns and balustrades. Enter, to be ushered by discreet staff into a cool lobby and up stairways to neat rooms decorated in soft tones with parquet floors. Pale gauze curtains frame tall windows overlooking the grounds or the therapy centre. The ballroom-like restaurant supports specialist diets and guests may use the spa pool and gym. The therapies are extra – worth every sou!

Hotel

rooms	43: 6 doubles, 8 twins, 9 triples, 2 family, 18 singles.
price	499 Kn-720 Kn. Singles 342 Kn-432 Kn. Full-board extra 58 Kn p.p. Half-price for children.
meals	Lunch/dinner 58 Kn.
closed	Never.
directions	On main road though Opatija following coast; south towards marina, Hotel on right, opp. Admiral Hotel.

	Sandra Martinčić
tel	+385 (0)51 202 680
fax	+385 (0)51 202 687
email	villa.dubrava@ri.t-com.hr
web	www.thalassotherapia-opatija.hr

Map 1 Entry 55

Hotel W.A. Mozart

M. Tita 138, Opatija, 51410 Primorje-Gorski Kotar

Many hotels in Croatia try to recreate the grandeur of the Austro-Hungarian empire; the Mozart pulls it off with style and a history to match. This is one of several listed Secessionist mansions that line the steep, wooded shoreline of Opatija. The ornamental and balconied façade is a delight and inside, public spaces invoke a world of elegance and grandeur with masses of polished reproduction furniture and ornate new upholstery. In the bedrooms, Deco-style bedsteads and peppermint-stripe chairs grace mahogany floors warmed with oriental rugs. Each room has its own columned balcony and views that sweep from the sea to the heavens. The dining room is a vision of Regency splendour; summer breakfasts are served in a secluded walled courtyard lush with plants. Opatija was the most fashionable of the Austro-Hungarian winter resorts in the 19th century, the air supposedly blessed with restorative qualities. The Mozart Hotel continues the restorative theme in its wellness centre – try a spot of holistic rebalancing or acupuncture, then take the sea air on the promenade. *Bikes available for hire.*

rooms	29: 21 doubles, 5 twins, 4 suites for 2, 3 or 4.
price	859 Kn-1,074 Kn. Singles 608 Kn-716 Kn. Suite 1,260 Kn-2,148 Kn. Half-board extra 120 Kn p.p.
meals	Lunch & dinner 120 Kn.
closed	Never.
directions	In centre of Opatija, opposite main beach. Detailed directions on booking.

	Dario Kinkela	Hotel
tel	+385 (0)51 718 260	
mobile	+385 (0)91 598 2251	
fax	+385 (0)51 271 877	
email	info@hotel-mozart.hr	
web	www.hotel-mozart.hr	

Map 1 Entry 56

Villa Astra

Viktora Cara Emina 11, Lovran, 51415 Primorje-Gorski Kotar

With its astonishing collection of gothic flourishes, balustrades and floral arches, this is an impressive address – even for Croatia's 'Riviera'. Vast rooms reveal harmonious colours, soft upholstery, paintings, sculptures and polished parquet: there's a sophisticated, neo-classical feel. From the upper floors, tall windows topped by trefoil arches look onto a duck-egg-blue infinity pool and a garden resplendent with magnolias, camellias and palms. At the foot of the grounds is a private sand and shingle beach lapped by Evian-clear waters. Nature trails snake along the shoreline and up into the hills. Many guests arrive by sea, transported from the airport on Krk in a speedboat-cloud of ocean spray. The restaurant promises fine dining with local ingredients selected to promote vitality; reflecting this trend, massage pavilions are planned for the waterfront. Considered one of the leading boutique hotels of the world, Villa Astra may not be quite as bohemian as it professes to be but to stay here is unadulterated delight. Hotelier Vjeko Martinko's empire extends to Farmhouse Oraj and Villa San Giovanni. *Bikes available for hire.*

Hotel

rooms	6 doubles.
price	€124–€129. Singles less 20%. Half-board €30 p.p.
meals	Dinner from 250 Kn.
closed	Mid-Nov–mid-Dec; mid-Jan–mid-Feb.
directions	From Zagreb & Rijeka, pass Opatija; cont. to Lovran (5km). At yellow sign for Lovran, before town, sign for Villa Astra; left up one-way street. Last house, opp. tennis court.

Anđelka Kosturin

tel	+385 (0)51 294 400
mobile	+385 (0)98 983 2425
fax	+385 (0)51 294 589
email	sales@lovranske-vile.com
web	www.lovranske-vile.com

Map 1 Entry 57

Villa San Giovanni

Šetalište Maršala Tita 45, Lovran, 51415 Primorje-Gorski Kotar

Gazing over the shores of the Liburnian coast – once the winter resort of the Austro-Hungarian nobility – Villa San Giovanni still exudes 19th-century gentility. Ceilings soar, elegant corridors lead from one beautifully styled room to the next, strokable upholsteries cover antique pieces and polished floorboards glide beneath your feet. With their slatted white shutters, these apartments make you feel as though you are staying in a discreet seaside retreat. The 'Green Residence' exhibits a classical Italianate style, all swirling rococo and curling opaque spirals; the 'Oriental' is a treasure house of Indonesian antiquities. Expect original art, baroque chandeliers and white muslin curtains; all is chic, elegant and impeccably finished. Living areas are spacious and stylish, with stretching corridors, grand bedrooms and thoughtfully designed kitchens; many rooms have balconies. Large gardens and shaded outdoor terraces are well-tended and enlivened by the yellow petunias so characteristic of the Lovranski-Vile marque, and the shingle beach and lapping waves are a step away.

rooms	3 apartments: 1 for 2, 1 for 4, 1 for 4-6.
price	€54–€206.
meals	Self-catering. Breakfast €14. Restaurants 1km.
closed	Never.
directions	From Lovran harbour, west along seafront down Šetalište Maršala Tita. Detailed directions on booking.

	Anđelka Kosturin	Self-catering
tel	+385 (0)51 294 604	
mobile	+385 (0)98 983 2425	
fax	+385 (0)51 294 589	
email	sales@lovranske-vile.com	
web	www.lovranske-vile.com	

Map 1 Entry 58

Farmhouse Oraj

Tuliševica 64, Lovran, 51415 Primorje-Gorski Kotar

Here is an eagles' eyrie, balanced on the slopes of Učka mountain, casting its gaze over the Opatija Riviera and the craggy island of Krk. Sheer natural beauty. With the sun's rays ricocheting off the sea, every view is astounding. Restored with diligence, this century-old farmhouse plays muse to artists and writers seeking inspiration away from Lovran's seaside bustle. Easels stand like sentries in the cellar while healing and horticultural tomes fill the library. Down in the kitchen, housekeepers Milica and Frane simmer handpicked ingredients on the stove: the mood is of homely indulgence. There are pictures on every wall and the sitting room has a Regency charm: humbug-striped chaises longues and divans, and sloping plastered ceilings. Surrounding the house are two and a half hectares of landscaped gardens, a hidden labyrinth and two historic caves – great prospects for children! Come, too, for special truffle-hunting weekends or to harvest cherries and asparagus in the fields and orchards. Then digest the fruits of your labours as the sun sets over brooding Krk island in the bay.

Catered villa & self-catering

rooms	Villa for 8.
price	€200–€400.
meals	Catered or self-catering. Restaurants within 5km.
closed	Never.
directions	From Lovran right before INA gas station. Follow signs for Tušilovica & Lovranska Draga. Continue towards Tušilovica until second sign for Oraj on left at curve, left on unpaved road to farm.

	Anđelka Kosturin
tel	+385 (0)51 294 604
mobile	+385 (0)98 983 2425
fax	+385 (0)51 294 589
email	sales@lovranske-vile.com
web	www.lovranske-vile.com

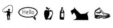

Map 1 Entry 59

Apartments Rukavina
Medveja 11b, Lovran, 51415 Primorje-Gorski Kotar

Mira Rukavina's tidy house appears to float on the hillside above the bay: a quiet spot with a grand view. Behind rise the slopes of Mount Učka, below is the beachfront, lined with tavernas offering barbecues of fish fresh from the bay. With its flower-filled gardens, rounded iron balustrades and white shuttered windows the house pays homage to the Hapsburgs. And behind the tall palm trees rustling in the breeze and the bright pink façade are two tidy apartments cared for by thoughtful Mira and her daughter. The top apartment (with an outside kitchen only) overlooks the winsome bay, the island of Krk dozing in the foreground, ringed by blue water. According to legend, this was the bay where Medea took refuge with Jason and his Golden Fleece; the sea at the base of the hill was formed from her tears when the object of her affections returned to his beloved Argonauts. Medveja retains a wistful air. The Rukavinas run the place like a second home and some guests have been coming here for 40 years. *Minimum stay three nights.*

rooms	2 apartments for 2-4.
price	280 Kn–490 Kn.
meals	Self-catering. Restaurants 200m.
closed	Never.
directions	From Opatija, 8km south to Medveja, then 70m northwards from main beach. Detailed directions on booking.

Self-catering

	Mira Rukavina
tel	+385 (0)51 291 159
mobile	+385 (0)98 831 987
email	mira.rukavina@ri.t-com.hr

Map 1 Entry 60

Apartman Tea
Risnjak 23, Crni Lug, 51317 Primorje-Gorski Kotar

Grey bears, wolves and lynx roam the wilds of Risnjak National Park – but you stand a better chance of spotting sparrowhawks, boar and deer... or finding a rare edelweiss. There are not many places to stay in the park but Apartman Tea has a prime position, being close to the visitor centre. It's a fine setting: in one direction, forested hills rise to the snowy peak of Veliki Risnja, in the other, green slopes slide down to the Adriatic. You have the best of both worlds, the mountains and the sea, and a comfortable chalet-like house from which to explore. The atmosphere is something between a ski cabin and a hunting lodge (you can ski and sledge in winter). Owners Jasenka and Josip live upstairs, while the roomy lower level is rented out as an apartment for four plus a fold-out bed. The 50s-style furniture may be dated but the apartment is bright and cheerful with a chintzy wooden bar in the living room. Josip hunts in the hills and sometimes brings back game – or you may tuck into local specialities in the restaurant near the park's headquarters. *Ask about photo safaris.*

Self-catering

rooms	Apartment for 4-5.
price	382 Kn-384 Kn.
meals	Self-catering. Park restaurant 10km.
closed	Never.
directions	A6 Zagreb-Rijeka, exit to Delnice. After 700m, left to Crni Lug. Follow signs for National Park. Apt just before park entrance, on right.

	Jasenka Turk
tel	+385 (0)51 836 212
mobile	+385 (0)98 941 3187
fax	+385 (0)51 836 212
email	ivana.malnar@ri.t-com.hr
web	www.apartman-tea.com

Map 1 Entry 61

Kuća Sobol

Kočićin bb, Kuželj, 51302 Primorje-Gorski Kotar

Five hundred species of butterfly flit around this mountain villa, resting in the natural gorge of the gently flowing Kupa. It's a classic mountain house – stone walls below, timber on top and attics extending the length of the barn-like roof. Croatians have been building houses like this for centuries but this one is new, as are most buildings in Kočićin; the original village was razed to the ground by the Italian occupation in WWII. The Restoration Institute of Rijeka supervised the rebuilding process so this is the real thing. You get a vast, stone-lined living room, a kitchen, two bedrooms (each with a double and a single bed), each with an extra bed, and two bathrooms, one surprisingly elaborate. One wood-panelled room has a ceiling lamp of antlers and a pair of traditional bedsteads; another follows the style of the coast: whitewashed walls, stone-framed windows, an antique dresser. The whole house is filled with family treasures; the living room could have stepped out of a museum of 19th-century village life. There's a terrace in the garden and you are surrounded by birds. *Minimum stay two to seven nights.*

rooms	House for 4-6.
price	€100–€140 per night.
meals	Self-catering.
	Restaurants within 5km.
closed	Never.
directions	From Rijeka, 50km northeast through Delnice to Brod na Kupi; 7km to Kočićin village.

Self-catering

	Alen & Silvija Sobol
tel	+385 (0)51 812 371
mobile	+385 (0)91 538 8552
email	alen.sobol@ri.htnet.hr
web	www.sobol.hr

Map 2 Entry 62

Coprnička hiša

Planina Skradska 43, Skrad, 51311 Primorje-Gorski Kotar

Perched on the edge of a mountain in Skrad, Coprnička hiša is a place for those in love with untamed nature. The house and its grassy, fruit tree'd garden climb the mountainside in a series of terraces; views of the surrounding hills are superb. Downhill – not far – is the lush natural park of Zeleni Vir (Green Whirlpool), criss-crossed by a series of easy walking trails and rugged scrambles through rocks and forest. It's an outdoorsy place, brilliant for younger groups looking for adventure (hiking and biking, rafting and riding) and with a few important 'luxuries' added: DVD and TV, fridge, barbecue and hob. The bedrooms – one twin, one triple – sleep up to five; there are a sitting room, a kitchen, a shower and two big terraces. Furniture is eclectic – a few family hand-me-downs – but comfortable, and the house stays cool in summer and is cosy in winter thanks to an open fire. Bojana Maričić or her cousin Robert meet guests on arrival and stop by once a week to clean and change sheets. Other than that, you are left alone to enjoy the wilderness. *30% supplement for under three nights.*

rooms	House for 5 (1 twin, 1 triple).
price	€75.
meals	Self-catering. Restaurants within 2km.
closed	Never.
directions	From Skrad, follow signs for Zeleni Vir. After 1km, left by drinking fountain, then right at the next crossing.

Self-catering

	Bojana Maričić
tel	+385 (0)51 277 278
mobile	+385 (0)91 539 0755
email	info@coprnicka-hisa.com
web	www.coprnicka-hisa.com

Map 2 Entry 63

Resting House Blaževci

Blaževci 5d, Vrbovsko, 51326 Primorje-Gorski Kotar

The name perfectly captures the charm of this pretty village house, overlooking the lazy Kupa river on the borders of Slovenia. Indeed, the river surrounds the place – a wooden bridge brings you to the front door, while the rocky slope behind is a perfect launch pad for canoes and inflatable boats. There's something very special about this island home: with flowers cascading from every balcony and window, it's the sort of place a fairy godmother might happily live. Inside are two good-sized bedrooms with sloping ceilings, a much smaller third bedroom under the roof, a modest bathroom and a kitchen (fully-equipped) that opens into the living room warmed by a cast-iron stove. The owner has made a real effort to create a homely feel here, so expect plenty of family knick-knacks. In the garden are a shaded gazebo, a barbecue and a bread oven – perfect for rustic dining. Nearby is Lukovdol, birthplace of the anti-war poet Ivan Goran Kovačić and the setting for a famous poetry festival every spring. You might just feel inspired to write a few sonnets yourself. *Bikes available for hire.*

rooms	Cottage for 6.
price	€100.
meals	Self-catering. Restaurants 3km.
closed	Never.
directions	From Zagreb, exit Vrbovsko, to Lukovdol; 7km to village.

Self-catering

	Zvonimir Muževič
tel	+385 (0)51 875 326
mobile	+385 (0)98 459 181
fax	+385 (0)51 875 326
email	dimnjak@inet.hr

Map 2 Entry 64

Kuća Leo

Breze, Ledenice, 51251 Primorje-Gorski Kotar

On a slope of silver birches and Mediterranean scrub, just above Novi Vinodolski, Breze was home once to 600 souls. Now there are five – but things liven up at weekends when outsiders pop by for a blast of mountain air. Nature abounds on all sides; the Velebit massif rises behind while a series of protected wildernesses straggle across the hills. The Butkovićs built their chalet in Alpine style, its pitched roof descending almost to the ground, in preparation for winter snows. In winter, feel wrapped in a blanket of warmth as logs crackle in the living room fireplace. In summer, the shutters open to forest views and cooling breezes. This is no palace, just a simple country home run by a charming young pair who live nearby, delighted to welcome you to this mountain eyrie. Two bedrooms, a bathroom, a kitchen and a living room – all you need. The area is of historic significance to Croatians: the Vinodolski Code was signed in Novi Vinodolski in 1288, limiting the power of the feudal lords, while Velebit is the legendary home of Vila Velebita, the guardian spirit of Kvarner. *Minimum stay four nights.*

Self-catering

rooms	House for 4.
price	€100–€120 per night.
meals	Self-catering. Restaurants within 10km.
closed	Never.
directions	From Rijeka, towards Novi Vinodolski. Follow signs for Breze. Ask for directions once you reach the saw-mill in the village.

	Igor Butković
tel	+385 (0)51 289 336
mobile	+385 (0)98 253 083
fax	+385 (0)51 289 336
email	gordana.butkovic@ri.t-com.hr

Map 2 Entry 65

Kuća Filipaši

Sv Jelena 15, Brseč, 51418 Primorje-Gorski Kotar

After the rows of plain boxy houses in the surrounding villages, Kuća Filipaši delighted us with its unexpected explosion of greenery and flowers. These two 200-year-old buildings have been restored with love by Ivan and Milica; Milica has adored the place since she was a child. Vine-covered pergolas cover paved terraces, cut stone appears around every corner and the garden is sweet with its rockery and cherry trees that burst with blossom every spring. Perhaps the most striking detail of the very striking cottage is its *tornjica*, a curving arched smokehouse that opens off the main living room, beautifully converted to fit a log fire and a hotplate for grilling. The cottage is rented out by the week, its kitchen far superior to those found in most holiday homes; the smaller stable can be used as a fourth bedroom or as a tiny, independent apartment. Rooms have quirky wooden furniture and wonky whitewashed walls with patches of exposed stone. Discover fishing villages, pebble beaches, and walking and biking trails by the score. *Minimum stay one week. Stables can be rented separately.*

rooms	Cottage for 8 (2 doubles, 1 twin; 1 double in stables).
price	€660–€1,200 per week.
meals	Self-catering. Restaurants within 4km.
closed	November–April.
directions	From Opatija, south towards Mošćenicka Draga; pass sign for Sv Jelena & Slamnjaki restaurant; 2nd right on asphalt road into hills.

	Milica Hrala
tel	+385 (0)51 291 8888
mobile	+385 (0)91 592 6419
email	vali19@net.hr
web	www.cottage-flora.com

Self-catering

Map 1 Entry 66

Tramontana

Beli, Cres Island, 51559 Primorje-Gorski Kotar

Carpeted with purple sage, Cres is the classic Adriatic island. When summer breezes blow, the air is scented with mountain herbs, while griffon vultures, protected by volunteers at the ecology centre in Beli, soar in the thermals overhead. Run with enthusiasm by Robert and Nina Malatestinić, the inn stands four-square above the ocean just outside the village with a stunning vista of islands, sea and sky. Built between the great wars, it has the feel of that age: it could be a field hospital out of *Captain Corelli's Mandolin*. The focus here is on marine adventure, particularly diving. Robert is a PADI-qualified scuba instructor and runs a full range of dive courses and fishing trips. Spending days together out at sea leads to a very jolly atmosphere back at the inn, particularly over a meal on the terrace restaurant, where seafood, organic meat and vegetables are often cooked over the embers of a wood fire. First-floor rooms, not luxurious but comfortable, are filled with space and light; windows have shutters and white curtains. Attic rooms are cosier, tucked beneath the beams.

Restaurant with rooms

rooms	6: 4 doubles, 2 family.
price	€50–€70. Half-board extra €11p.p.
meals	Dinner around €11.
	Packed lunch €5.
	A la carte, with wine, €5–€25.
closed	January-February.
directions	Ferry to Cres island. Follow only road 20km; left to Beli. Signs to guest house.

Robert Malatestinić

tel	+385 (0)51 840 519
mobile	+385 (0)99 216 5010
fax	+385 (0)51 840 519
email	pansion-tramontana@ri.t-com.hr
web	www.diving-beli.com

Map 1 Entry 67

Manora Hotel

Mandalenska 26b, Nerezine, Lošinj Island, 51554 Primorje-Gorski Kotar

The Manora could have been sculpted from fondant icing. Each of its four cubes is painted a brilliant shade of white, yellow or blue, broken up by tall shuttered windows. Inside is equally modern. Rooms are decorated in pastel shades of yellow, blue and red – you could be living in a minimalist painting. Those who have a penchant for bold modern design, calm spaces and deep comfort will be very happy. Choose a room to suit your mood – yellow for positive thinking, red for passion, blue for cool energy. Each one is named after an Adriatic ship, its picture framed by the door. Far and away the most striking hotel on Lošinj Island, Manora sits on the shoulder of Mount Orošćica and is linked to the pebble beach and azure waters by a winding path. Despite the boutique concept – conceived by a relative of the owners – this is still very much a family-run, hands-on affair. Outside is a gorgeous swimming pool surrounded by dapper wooden loungers, and the warm red restaurant specialises in the herb-fed lamb for which these gorgeous islands are famous. *Bikes available for hire.*

rooms	22 doubles.
price	€78–€136. Singles €47–€82.
meals	Lunch & dinner around €30.
closed	Never.
directions	Ferry to Merag on Cres. 60km south dir. Mali Lošinj; hotel on right, after Nerezine, 15km before Mali Lošinj. Owners can arrange transport from Rijeka airport on Krk.

Hotel

	Roland Spišić
tel	+385 (0)51 237 460
mobile	+385 (0)98 329 608
fax	+385 (0)51 237 470
email	manora@manora-losinj.hr
web	www.manora-losinj.hr

Map 1 Entry 68

KADO Resort & Spa

Brzac 85, Malinska, Krk Island, 51511 Primorje-Gorski Kotar

These architecturally striking apartments have been styled with imagination. In one bedroom, a giant rose emerges from behind the headboard, in another, two large daisies stretch to the ceiling. The capacious one-bedroom suites (extra beds available) have graceful wrought-iron bedsteads and eye-catching murals by Croatian artist Đurđica Merle; colours and shapes have been thoughtfully considered, living rooms have been dressed in rustic fabrics and cushions tossed into every corner. Those with a penchant for contemporary design will love it. Masses of outside space too: balconies with views of the island of Cres, shared decks protected by curvaceous stone walls, green seating areas and a super grill bar. Wooden benches surround a hidden hot tub and in front of the main house are two gorgeous pools – one for adults, one for small children. Indoor's water features are equally enticing: fabulous shower rooms have underfloor lighting. Then there's the sauna, the restaurant, the massage spa... and the welcome, which is big. Great for couples and young families. *30% supplement for under three nights. Bikes available for hire.*

Self-catering resort

Map 1 Entry 69

rooms	13 apartments: 12 for 2-4, 1 for 2-3.
price	€150–€200.
meals	Self-catering. Breakfast €5. Lunch & dinner €15.
closed	Never.
directions	Cross Krk bridge, follow signs for Krk town. At sign to Valbiska, right for Glavotok; thro' Linardici. In Milohnic, sign to Glavotok & Brzac; enter Brzac, sign to Glavotok. Resort signed.

Krešimir Pavić

tel	+385 (0)51 862 082
mobile	+385 (0)91 338 3381
fax	+385 (0)51 862 084
email	info@apartmani-krk.net
web	www.apartmani-krk.net

Villa Rustica

Sv Ivan Dobrinjski 42, Dobrinj, Krk Island, 51514 Primorje-Gorski Kotar

There are few road signs and confusing house numbers in the old stone village of Sv Ivan Dobrinjski – but persevere. The once dilapidated house is the epitome of comfortable country living: a heart-warming jumble of stone arches, warm tiles and topped chimneys. Blue shutters and whitewashed walls create a Provençal feel, mirrored by the blue pool below the terrace and the open sea beyond. You rent the house by the week – two roomy bedrooms, a country-style living room and kitchen, lawns, terrace, pool. Bedrooms have large beds and are full of light and rustic details – ancient beams, stone-framed windows, pretty muslin. Floors are neatly tiled and antiques glow; a stained-glass window and wrought-iron wall lanterns add a medieval touch. Not a sound at night from the little village, just the hoot of a Mediterranean owl. Quite a few of the houses here are holiday homes, restored by Croatians who fell in love with the island and stayed. The grounds are peaceful and wooden, the lovely beach is a walk away. *Minimum stay four nights (one week July/August).*

rooms	Villa for 4.
price	€750–€1,500 per week.
meals	Self-catering. Restaurants 3km.
closed	November–March.
directions	From Rijeka airport, 14km towards Klimno, off Krk road. Tricky to find, detailed directions on booking.

	Marija & Dušan Mijić
tel	+385 (0)51 868 110
mobile	+45 (0)21 494 449 Dušan
	+385 (0)91 529 9632 Marija
email	dusan@qtours.dk
web	www.villa-rustica.com

Self-catering

Map 1 Entry 70

Hotel Kanajt

Kanajt 5, Punat, 51521 Primorje-Gorski Kotar

Founded in 1528 as a summer palace for the bishops of Krk, the grand *rezidenca* on the shores of Punat Bay has not lost its air of ecclesiastical calm. Today's visitors arrive in sailing blues, directly from the marina outside. Set back from the water among lawns and trees, the green-shuttered mansion is somewhat incongruously topped by a rooftop sign from the pre-war years. Front windows face the white masts of the yachts lined up on the water; back rooms overlook the excavated ruins of a church surrounded by olive grove. The manager Ivan Žic and his wife Iva give a professional welcome, steering new arrivals upstairs to classically-styled rooms that envelop you in warm pastel colours. Some have private terraces. Yachtsmen sometimes put up here: it's a comfortable place in which to find your legs before setting off for supper in the marina. The village of Punat dozes quietly for most of the year, and is charming; things are quieter still on Košljun Island, just across the bay. Dominated by a Franciscan monastery, it has its own library and museum.

rooms	21: 14 doubles, 6 twins, 1 suite.
price	€60–€160.
meals	Restaurants 300m.
closed	Never.
directions	Over bridge from mainland; 30km south dir. Punat; 30m after the sign for Punat, 1st on left; hotel on right opp. marina.

Hotel

	Iva Žic
tel	+385 (0)51 654 340
fax	+385 (0)51 654 341
email	info@kanajt.hr
web	www.kanajt.hr

Map 1 Entry 71

Hotel & Winery Boškinac
Novaljsko Polje b.b., Novalja, Pag Island, 53291 Lika-Senj

The Boškinac winery has the feel of a Roman villa – a tall, terracotta topped country house, fronted by columns and surrounded by vineyards; which is fitting: the island is littered with Roman remains. Pag is one of the less familiar Croatian islands, a parched but beautiful strip of land covered in strangely eroded rocks and Mediterranean scrub, and blessed with sand beaches. It is famous among locals for lace and a particularly pungent kind of goats' cheese – you'll surely be invited to try some during your stay. Boškinac Winery spills across a hillside above Novalja, the main resort, producing distinctive whites from the gegić grape. Boris Šuljić and Mirela Šanko have done a fine job here, creating something classic from new materials. All you see is brand new, but in sympathy with the architectural traditions of the island. Inside, photos, paintings and dried flowers create the feel of an old country vineyard. Rooms are styled with colours representing the seasons, interestingly upholstered soft furnishings and subtle lighting. Choose a suite if you wish to spread out.

rooms	11: 4 doubles, 4 twins, 3 suites for 3.
price	€100–€200. Singles €80–€150. Suite €140–€230. Half-board extra €27 p.p. Full-board extra €54 p.p.
meals	Lunch and dinner from 190 Kn.
closed	January.
directions	From Novalja, follow signs for Stara Novalja; barrels & sign mark the turning to hotel.

Mirela Šanko

tel	+385 (0)53 663 500
mobile	+385 (0)91 663 5001
fax	+385 (0)53 663 501
email	info@boskinac.com
web	www.boskinac.com

Hotel

Map 6 Entry 72

Dalmatia: kaleidoscope of the Adriatic

One of the Mediterranean's most naturally gorgeous regions is the coastline of Northern and Central Dalmatia. The deep blue waters of the Adriatic, strewn with rugged islands and remote crags, is a photographer's dream. Dotted around both mainland and islands are dozens of unspoiled beaches and historic cities, while the channels between the islands are served by the summer Maestral winds, ideal for windsurfers and sailors.

The islands can be treated as self-contained entities and many people base their trips on just one, getting around by scooter, hire car, water taxi or boat. The towns on the mainland, too, have rich treasures – and there are the Krka Falls, tumbling magically over a series of ledges near Skradin.

Partly eclipsed by Dubrovnik to the south, Dalmatia's official capital, Split, is majestic. The Emperor Diocletian made his home here; it is now one of the most perfectly preserved Roman palaces in the world.

Not far from here, enchanting Trogir is a fortified city on a tomb-shaped island, crafted from pale white stone and framed by the channels that separate the mainland from the island of Čiovo. Skinny bridges link the islands to the new town, forming a sheltered mooring for some of the Adriatic's sleekest yachts.

South of Trogir, a string of remote lighthouses protects the channels between the islands in the bay. Many are open to paying guests who don't mind forgoing a few creature comforts for the romance of the setting. The closest holiday island to Trogir is Brač, source of the white stone used to build medieval towns all along the coast. Near the elegant resort of Bol is Croatia's most iconic (shingle) beach, Zlatni Rat, singularly beautiful and a mecca for yachties and windsurfers.

Hvar is considered one of the ten most beautiful islands in the world. Hvar Town, chic, atmospheric and car-free, is rich with monuments and home to some fabulously good restaurants.

Back on the mainland, Zadar is the gateway to the national parks of Dalmatia; five lie within an hour of the city. Dominated by medieval fortifications, this is also the leaping-off point for the 150 islets, islands and reefs of the Kornati archipelago. This barren wonderland of karst and undiscovered beaches and coves is a dedicated national park and a place of humbling serenity.

The sleepy island of Vis was, until recently, home to a military base, which helped preserve its quiet atmosphere. The marine life here is among the richest and least plundered in Croatia (you'll even find the odd sunken ship) and the island's peaceful guest houses and villas are proving an increasing draw for a fashionable crowd.

Photo Kathryn Tomasetti

Hotel President

Vladana Desnice 16, Zadar Borik, 23000 Zadar

Croatia's Austro-Hungarian past is evident in this swanky new city hotel. The décor shows off the effusive Biedermeier style, so fashionable in Vienna between the Napoleonic Wars and the uprisings of the 1840s. There's plenty of bourgeois extravagance here, and the elegance of the service matches the styling; if you're not a high-flyer, you'll be treated like one. Fabrics are rich to the touch, curtains are elaborately hung and bathrooms swim with marble, their fittings courtesy of Villeroy & Boch. Bedroom sofas and armchairs are decorated in Regency stripes; some pieces were created from cherrywood by artisans in Slovenia. Classical music leads one to the Vivaldi Restaurant, where the meals are operatic compositions, beautifully presented and served with a judiciously chosen list of Croatian and international wines. Technology hums behind the scenes: each room has an internet connection and a fax machine for those who mix business with leisure. The hotel has an excellent position in the Borik district, away from the centre of Zadar but rather handy for the plush yachts moored in Borik's marina. *Bikes available for hire.*

Hotel

rooms	27: 12 doubles, 3 singles, 12 suites.
price	998 Kn-1,608 Kn.
	Singles 890 Kn-1,371 Kn.
	Suites 1,740 Kn-2,799 Kn.
	Half-board extra 220 Kn p.p.
meals	Lunch & dinner 250 Kn-300 Kn.
	Restaurants 150m.
closed	Never.
directions	A1 Zagreb-Split, exit Maslenica; 20 mins. to Zadar. Take Cesta Hrvatskog Sabora ring road, or enter city via Jadranska cesta. Signed.

	Zdravko Barbarosa
tel	+385 (0)23 333 696
fax	+385 (0)23 333 595
email	info@hotel-president.hr
web	www.hotel-president.hr

Map 6 Entry 73

Prišnjak Lighthouse
Prišnjak Island, Šibenik-Knin

Looking almost like a seaside cottage – apart from the tower emerging from the sea-facing wall – the lighthouse was built in 1886 to protect trading vessels that plied the channels between Zadar and Šibenik. Prišnjak Island is as remote and wild as any on this coast, but the joy of this setting is that the island of Murter, with its clutchful of pretty coastal resorts, is 25 minutes by boat and trips can be arranged with Severin Kulušić whenever you like. A never-ending source of sea-faring yarns, the charismatic Captain also settles you into your simple but adequate quarters. Prišnjak's appeal is privacy – an island to yourself – and the views at sunset and sunrise from your own little beach are something to treasure. What's more, the waters are shallow, with steps in for children, and reach bath-like temperatures in summer: bliss for families. An aged pine tree close by gives the best shade on the island; below is a barbecue on which you may find yourself cooking something tasty caught moments before. *Minimum stay seven nights in summer. No heating.*

rooms	Apartment for 4.
price	€729–€1,099 per week.
meals	Self-catering. Bring provisions; fish available at extra charge. Shops on Murter.
closed	Never.
directions	Transfer from Murter (25 mins/€60) at any time of day.

	Adriatica.net
tel	+44 (0)20 7183 0437
fax	+385 (0)1 245 2909
email	info@adriatica.net
web	www.adriatica.net

Lighthouse

Map 6 Entry 74

Hotel Skradinski Buk

Burinovac b.b., Skradin, 22222 Šibenik-Knin

As it rushes through the forests of Krka National Park, the river spills into seven mighty waterfalls before reaching the Roman town of Skradin; the final falls are the most spectacular. Skradinski Buk is one of Croatia's most famous beauty spots, an amazing mass of churning, frothing waters framed by forest. You can reach the Falls via a riverside trail or take a boat from the quayside in town. In summer, half the town will be here, swimming peacefully or careering down the slides formed by the smaller cascades. Named after the Falls, the Skradinski Buk is a neat, modern hotel painted in friendly shades of pink and orange, floodlit at night. Inside, bedrooms and public spaces are more hotel-tidy than characterful, with cheerful colours and much comfort. The suites would be perfect for families. The inviting dining room has red chairs and some rough stone walls; eggshell blue sofas sit in the carpeted bar; friendly, efficient staff serve you. The town is worth exploring and Krka National Park is everything it's cracked up to be. A super little place.

Hotel

rooms	29: 6 doubles, 17 twins, 4 singles, 2 suites for 2 (extra beds for children).
price	€51–€81. Half-board €34–€49 per person. 30% discount for children sharing suite.
meals	55 Kn-150 Kn.
closed	Never.
directions	Follow signs to Skradin, past the bridge on Krka river and left at the crossing, following signs to hotel.

	Marijana Pulić
tel	+385 (0)22 771 771
mobile	+385 (0)99 205 1975
fax	+385 (0)22 771 770
email	skradinski-buk@si.t-com.hr
web	www.skradinskibuk.hr

Map 6 Entry 75

Hotel Maestral

Prvić Luka, Prvić Island, 22233 Šibenik-Knin

There is just enough space for two teacup-sized villages on tiny Prvić, and you can walk between them in ten minutes. The first visitors were hermits in search of meditative serenity, and there is still a peaceful air, with all cars prohibited. Hotel Maestral takes its name from the maestral wind, the balmy northwestern breeze that blows between the islands on hot summer afternoons. The hotel is just metres from the pier and spills out onto the main town square. In the island's heyday, the hotel was a school, and there's still a Mediterranean schoolhouse feel – you can imagine the children staring through the shuttered windows, daydreaming about diving off the seawall after the final bell. In the winter, owner Filip works as a photo journalist for an American newspaper; in the summer, he oversees the running of the hotel with his wife and four daughters. Bedrooms are above the restaurant and are a perfect mix of traditional and contemporary – neatly pointed stonework, polished timbers, pale minimalist furnishings. Come for comfort and blissful tranqullity.

rooms	12: 11 twins, 1 suite for 2-4.
price	€46–€90. Suite €75–€135.
meals	Lunch & dinner around €10.
closed	Never.
directions	From Sibenik or Vodice, ferry to Prvić Luka. Left from jetty; hotel 20m on left.

	Filip Horvat	Hotel
tel	+385 (0)22 448 300	
fax	+385 (0)22 448 301	
email	info@hotelmaestral.com	
web	www.hotelmaestral.com	

Map 6 Entry 76

Zlatna Ribica

Krapanjskih spužvara 46, Brodarica, 22010 Šibenik-Knin

The village of Brodarica is blessed by the mix of fresh and salt water in the bay: a perfect environment for spawning fish, shells and sponges. There's still some diving for sponges off nearby Krapanj Island. This is one of the quieter spots on the coast near Split – but don't worry, Vesna Tudić makes up for it with her huge personality. The Tudić family ventured into tourism half a century ago, with a modest family restaurant on the harbour front. Now Zlatna Ribica is a busy waterside hotel. Slick and modern from the outside, it is warmly human inside, its wooden floors and simple artworks creating a peaceful atmosphere in the rooms. The hotel sprawls over several pink houses beside the marina, its hub the restaurant still. Not only do they serve local specialities and wines from the nearby family vineyard, they also host food festivals. Internet access and a well-equipped fitness centre are included in the price, and a shuttle boat runs regularly between the harbour and Krapanj – worth a visit for its monastery musuem outlining the history of the sponge divers.

rooms	16 + 3: 16 doubles. 3 apartments for 3.
price	€48. Singles €34. Apartments €60–€90.
meals	Lunch & dinner €14.
closed	Never.
directions	From Šibenik, 5km south towards Trogir. Turn off to Zlatna Ribica. Signed on right.

Hotel & Self-catering

	Vesna Tudić Dodić
tel	+385 (0)22 350 695
fax	+385 (0)22 351 877
email	tudic@si.t-com.hr
web	www.zlatna-ribica.hr

Map 6 Entry 77

Krknjaši

Drvenik Veliki, 21245 Split-Dalmatia

Guarding the channel between Ćiovo and Šolta, the island of Drvenik Veli is low and lush, skirted by rocks and pebble beaches and topped by a tangle of olive trees and aromatic Mediterranean shrubs. This is a small, self-contained isle, home to just 145 people, proud of their relaxed, island way of life. Looking out over a sandy bay in the southeast and protected by two small islets, Krknjaši Resort started as a restaurant for lunchtime bathers from visiting yachts and slowly expanded into a lovely getaway. Don't be misled by the word 'resort' – this is an island stay at its most natural and unselfconscious. From the jetty, a stone path leads up through an ancient olive grove to a cluster of stone houses with shady tiled terraces. Ivica Špika has created a wonderfully languorous mood: cottage walls are a patchwork of stone, simple wooden furniture mirrors the beams and floorboards, and the scent of sea spray and wild sage wafts in through the lace-curtained windows. There's a green ethic, too – rainwater showers, locally-caught fish and vegetables grown in the garden. *Minimum stay four nights.*

rooms	9 cottages: 8 for 2, 1 for 4.
price	Half-board €240.
meals	Half-board only. Lunch & dinner 40 Kn–120 Kn.
closed	October-May.
directions	Ferry from Split to Veliki Drvenik (6nm/11.2km). Resort on south-east side of island, 3km. Call for directions.

	Dragica Špika
tel	+385 (0)21 893 073
mobile	+385 (0)91 575 0925
fax	+385 (0)21 884 000
email	ivica.spika@st.t-com.hr
web	www.krknjasi.com

Resort

Map 6 Entry 78

Villa Sv Petar

Ivana Duknovića 14, Trogir, 21220 Split-Dalmatia

If you like your modern comforts tinged with Renaissance charm, delve into the alleyways behind the Cathedral of Sv Ivan in old Trogir. Here stands Villa Sv Petar, a 700-year-old townhouse recently and elegantly updated by Verner Hrnikaš, his wife Taida and her brother Mišo. Wherever possible, the original materials have been kept – stone walls, wooden shutters, wrought-iron – while the old flagstones on the ground floor were lifted, cleaned and painstakingly relaid. The result is a house that shines as it did in its heyday. In the bedrooms, a clean, uncluttered look prevails. Exposed stone walls and mahogany floors are complemented by smart contemporary furniture and long white curtains. Bathrooms are compact but spotless; shuttered windows look over Sv Petar's Church and the oldest building in Trogir, the former home of Nicolo of Florence. Wake to church bells, and the soft light reflected off white limestone walls. For advice on the area, turn to Mišo: he has years of experience in the tourist industry and a huge enthusiasm for the history of Trogir.

rooms	4 + 1: 4 doubles. 1 apartment for 3-4.
price	550 Kn-660 Kn. Apartment 803 Kn-902 Kn.
meals	Breakfast 50 Kn p.p. for self-catering guests. Restaurants 50m.
closed	Never.
directions	25km westwards up coast from Split, 10km from airport. In centre of Old Town, behind Sv Petar's Church.

B&B & self-catering

	Mišo Stergar Calebotta
tel	+385 (0)21 884 359
fax	+385 (0)21 884 359
email	sv.petar@hi.t-com.hr
web	www.villa-svpetar.com

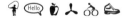

Map 7 Entry 79

Sv. Osib

Hotel Sikaa

Obala Kralja Zvonimira 13, Trogir, 21220 Split-Dalmatia

An eye-pleasing jumble of stone fortifications and Florentine church spires, Trogir is one of those lovely Croatian towns that define the Dalmatian coast. Hotel Sikaa has guarded the bridge between watery Trogir and the rugged island of Čiovo for over 300 years. A listed monument, it faces directly onto the channel, giving a snapshot view of the Old Town from its charming façade. Run with an easy-going professionalism by the Runtić family, the hotel promises old-fashioned comfort. There's a traditional, polished feel, from wooden floors, flowing curtains and historic prints on walls. Seven of the rooms overlook the city and its church towers, shuttered mansions and sleek yachts coursing between the two islands. The pricier rooms are the most cosseting, with saunas, jacuzzis and hydromassage showers. As it's a small hotel, staff can give a personal service, while communal tables at breakfast and a wood-panelled bar encourage guests to meet. Breakfasts are a spread – omelettes, homemade cakes, breads, cereals, yogurt, cheeses and excellent coffee. A pleasing little place, in a stunning setting.

rooms	10: 8 doubles, 2 twins.
price	500 Kn-800 Kn. Singles 470 Kn-750 Kn.
meals	Restaurants 1km.
closed	Never.
directions	From Old Town, over bridge to Čiovo Island (150m). Right onto main road; hotel immediately on left.

	Stjepan Runtić	Hotel
tel	+385 (0)21 798 240	
mobile	+385 (0)98 370 590	
fax	+385 (0)21 885 149	
email	info@vila-sikaa-r.com	
web	www.vila-sikaa-r.com	

Map 7 Entry 80

Hotel Pašike

Sinjska bb, Trogir, 21220 Split-Dalmatia

The Buble family have filled their 500-year-old hotel with much-loved antiques and their staff wear traditional Dalmatian costume. Frankica and Mate Buble pull it all off with charm and good humour. You can understand their enthusiasm for history – the hotel is hidden down a cobbled backstreet in Trogir's enchanting Old Town, surrounded by Renaissance towers. It has been in the family for 300 years and much of the furniture has been passed down the generations. Bedrooms are lovely, traditional but with a fresh feel, lit by large windows, enhanced by light timber floors and an uncluttered display of period dressers, wardrobes and beds. Patterns of stonework peek through the plaster, and the top-floor terrace has a stork's eye view over ancient rooftops. Historic charm combines with modern convenience: wi-fi, air conditioning, satellite TV. The restaurant's chefs are on a mission to rediscover the lost foods of Dalmatia and all sorts of delicious and unusual dishes appear on the menu – accompanied by a Trogir folk band most evenings in summer. *10% supplement for stays of under three nights.*

rooms	8: 7 twins, 1 suite.
price	700 Kn. Singles 550 Kn. Suite 1,100 Kn. Half-board extra 59 Kn p.p. Full-board extra 118 Kn p.p.
meals	Breakfast 50 Kn. Lunch & dinner 70 Kn.
closed	Never.
directions	Drive west along northern edge of Old Town. Hotel well signed.

Hotel

	Frankica & Mate Buble
tel	+385 (0)21 881 629
mobile	+385 (0)91 584 8434
fax	+385 (0)21 797 729
email	info@hotelpasike.com
web	www.hotelpasike.com

Map 7 Entry 81

Hotel Tragos
Budislavićeva 3, Trogir, 21220 Split-Dalmatia

There are historic hotels – and there is Hotel Tragos. According to a carved stone above the entrance, it has been standing since 1275. The old house expanded into a stately baroque palace in the 18th century; today, along with many others in Trogir's Old Town, the building is UNESCO-protected. Apart from an attractively contemporary makeover, little has changed since the 1780s; ancient walls are punctuated by tiny shutters that still reveal old stone walls and canopies of beams. The décor is less traditional. Rooms are fresh, uncluttered and modern, with pale pine sofas and beds, fabrics in warm sunshiny colours and scatter rugs on floors. Bathrooms display big cream and black tiles; some have tubs, others just showers; all are a cut above the average. Jerko Žunić has found an energetic and enthusiastic staff to back him; this is a well-run place. For meals you have a pretty sun terrace and a charming stone-clad restaurant serving authentic Dalmatian dishes, spilling onto a second ivy-draped terrace behind. And what a position – 20 metres from the main square in Trogir.

rooms	12: 1 double, 4 twins, 7 triples.
price	€82–€110. Singles €62–€82. Half-board & full-board extra €12–€22 p.p.
meals	Lunch & dinner around €25.
closed	Never.
directions	E65 exit Trogir; past bus station on left & over stone bridge to Old Town; parking on right. Walk thro' main gate, left past cathedral, right at main square; 2nd street on left.

Hotel

	Jerko Žunić
tel	+385 (0)21 884 729
mobile	+385 (0)98 982 5406
fax	+385 (0)21 884 731
email	info@tragos.hr
web	www.tragos.hr

Map 7 Entry 82

Water Mill Pantan

Pantan bb, Trogir, 21220 Split-Dalmatia

Everyone loves a watermill: the solid, functional architecture, the trickle of water from the stream. Water Mill Pantan is all a traditional mill should be – a robust stone tower on a duck-filled millpond, built in the 16th century to grind the corn from the fields around Trogir. Josip Pavić bought it for a change of pace, having worked for years as a doctor in America. With his wife Mendiana, he has transformed a place of industry into a delightful place to unwind. The setting is flawless, surrounded by a pristine nature reserve with 196 species of wild birds. You can walk in the water meadows or take lazy excursions on the family boat, following the bullrush-fringed river down to the sea near Trogir. The bedrooms, slightly austere, are in perfect keeping with the building; stone walls, pure white linen and pale wooden furniture create a feeling of cleanliness and space. Rather than ignoring the river, the couple have invited it into the house; water charges and churns under a glass floor in the *konoba*, where fine Dalmatian food is served along with delicious home-baked bread.

rooms	3 doubles.
price	€50–€70.
meals	Breakfast €7. Lunch & dinner €15.
closed	Never.
directions	From Trogir, 3km towards Split, signed on right.

Restaurant with rooms

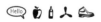

	Mendiana Pavić
tel	+385 (0)21 895 095
mobile	+385 (0)95 905 6890
fax	+385 (0)21 882 330
email	doctorpavic@hotmail.com
web	www.pantan.hr

Map 7 Entry 83

Villa Lavandula

Put Salduna 3, Čiovo Island, Trogir, 21220 Split-Dalmatia

Bon viveurs live like millionaires in this Deco-inspired mansion at the western end of Čiovo Island. Josip Pavković's taste for life's luxuries is evident from the jacuzzi on the terrace, the fully-equipped fitness suite and sauna and the 15-metre luxury yacht bobbing in the bay. A few years ago he transformed his home into six self-catering apartments, decorated in warm, soothing colours, with swish modern furniture, designer bathrooms and large family photographs in sepia gracing the walls. The nearest beaches are right below the house on scenic Saldrun bay, but the family also owns an idyllic private beach at the tip of the island, a ten-minute drive away. Other treats include island tours, visits to the family ranch and excursions on the family yacht. Josip is an enthusiastic raconteur and evenings often end on the terrace with Cuban cigars, tall tales and a glass of home-distilled grappa. He also takes care of the cooking, turning out sophisticated Dalmatian dishes that use only ingredients from local farms and markets. *Secure parking.*

rooms	6 apartments: 1 for 2, 1 for 3, 1 for 5, 3 for 6.
price	Apartments €90–€150.
meals	Self-catering. Breakfast €10. Lunch & dinner from €25.
closed	Never.
directions	From Trogir, cross 2nd bridge to Čiovo island. Turn right, 1km on main road sign for Villa Lavandula.

Self-catering

	Josip Pavković
tel	+385 (0)21 798 330
mobile	+385 (0)91 264 7711
fax	+385 (0)21 798 331
email	villa@villalavandula.com
web	www.villalavandula.com

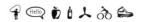

Map 7 Entry 84

Vila Dolce Vita

Miševac 18, Čiovo Island, Trogir, 21220 Split-Dalmatia

Behind the simple, modern façade lie unexpected comforts. Perched high, overlooking the channel between Čiovo Island and Croatia, these self-catering apartments are attractively proportioned inside and topped by a roof terrace with views of hills, sea and sky. For outdoorsy types, the forest begins almost from the door; for the languid, there's an outdoor pool with hydromassage jets and loungers. The charming old town of Trogir lies a few kilometres along the shore. The owners are continually upgrading the building and adding new features – a terrace here, a winter garden there. They met in Austria, where Dragana's family took refuge during the recent war, and returned in peacetime. Both are enthusiastic and involved, with Roman conjuring up Dalmatian and Austrian meals using organic produce from the family farm. Most of the apartments have balconies and the interiors are fresh and new – clean modern furniture and big beds topped by starched linen. Bathrooms have a nautical theme and water is heated by solar panels. *Minimum stay five nights July/August.*

Self-catering

rooms	9 apartments: 4 for 3, 4 for 4, 1 for 6.
price	€30–€100. Air-conditioning €5 per room.
meals	Self-catering. Breakfast €6. Meals optional.
closed	Never.
directions	From Trogir Old Town cross to Čiovo Island. Signed off main road.

	Roman & Dragana Schloegl
tel	+385 (0)21 888 164
mobile	+385 (0)98 196 6544
email	info@vila-dolcevita.com
web	www.vila-dolcevita.com

Map 7 Entry 85

Apartmani Marije
Priora Petra 8 and Obrov 10, Split, 21000 Split-Dalmatia

You'd think you'd pay a fortune to stay among the Renaissance churches, Venetian piazzas and Roman ruins of old Split. Not a bit of it. Neighbours Ante Runjić and Gordana Kulušić own two charming houses in the heart of the city, whose rooms you may rent at a very reasonable price. The old stone buildings stand just metres from the Diocletian's Palace – an amazing position. Communal space is limited but the bedrooms are a delight – compact and colourful, with wooden floors and shared or en suite bathrooms with Croatian 'deep showers' (half shower, half tub). Windows look onto cobbled streets and stone piazzas – perfect for people-watching over cups of coffee, and watching the comings and goings of the local fish market. Ante and Gordana, she quiet and thoughtful, he a whirlwind of energy, have been friends since childhood; if one house is full they pass guests on to the other. After welcoming you and settling you in they leave you to your own devices, but are always ready with advice when you need it. Don't miss the Diocletian's Palace, for its state rooms, Roman walls *and* luscious boutiques.

rooms	9 + 1: 4 doubles, 4 twins, 1 triple, some sharing bathrooms. 1 apartment for 2.
price	€40-€70. Singles €40-€70. Triple €90. Apartment €50.
meals	Breakfast not available. Restaurants 200m.
closed	Never.
directions	From Split Harbour, west along waterfront; on Marmontova, turn left onto Kraj Sv Marije, right to Obrov.

Rooms & Self-catering

	Gordana Kulušić
tel	+385 (0)21 332 303
mobile	+385 (0)98 969 7129
fax	+385 (0)21 332 304
email	krsto.kulusic@st.htnet.hr
web	www.jadrantours.com/denis

Map 7 Entry 86

Base Sobe

Kraj Svetog Ivana 3, Split, 21000 Split-Dalmatia

Not many houses back onto the ruins of a Roman temple. Reached via alleyways inside the Diocletian's Palace, Base Sobe wraps you in history. Some parts of the building go back as far as the third century AD – the side wall formed part of the Temple of Jupiter – and the newest parts are 250 years old. It's a special backdrop for some unusually upbeat design. Tina Šarić and friends first established a small art gallery on the ground floor, then created three comfortable guest rooms above. Bold colours and curves contrast with open stonework, natural fabrics and polished parquet. Each room has its own character, the most striking with its basin sunk into an antique wooden cabinet; all have underfloor heating in their bathrooms and computers with internet access (extra charge). The handsome stone house combines the best of new and old in historic Split, and Tina is an energetic, creative and engaging hostess. There's no space for a breakfast room or sitting room here, but you won't mind a bit: restaurants, galleries, coffee shops and bars wait to be discovered.

Rooms

rooms	3 twins/doubles.
price	€60–€70.
meals	Breakfast not available. Restaurants 100m.
closed	Never.
directions	In centre of Old Town. With your back to tourist office behind Jupiter's Temple, left across the square to small alley, Kraj Svetog Ivana. Guest house signed on right.

	Tina Šarić
tel	+385 (0)21 483 195
mobile	+385 (0)98 735 137
email	mail@base-rooms.com
web	www.base-rooms.com

Map 7 Entry 87

Hotel Vestibul Palace

Iza vestibula 4, Split, 21000 Split-Dalmatia

Named after the vestibule in the heart of Diocletian's Palace — what a site — the hotel is a landmark in Split. Formed by the joining of three palaces — one Gothic, one Roman, one Renaissance — some of the walls go back to the third century. Immediately behind is the Vestibule itself, a grand wing of the emperor's apartments, once domed, now open to the sky. Owner Vladimir Smoje is rightly proud of his stylish hotel, and his staff couldn't be more helpful. The mood is luxurious, cosseting, packed with fine detail, the styling contemporary, the living spaces beautifully designed. Some walls are white, others present a field of natural stone, offset by charcoal curtains and bedspreads and square angles. One of the suites is a huge open chamber, its bed floating on a white column above a private sitting room reached via a spiral wooden stair. Elsewhere are light-filled atriums and a restaurant displaying equal panache. The food is a modern take on Croatian classics. Seven perfect rooms, all the technology you need — plasma screens in the suites, internet and satellite TV; this is a treat for the design-savvy.

rooms	7: 5 doubles, 2 suites for 4.
price	From €190.
meals	Lunch & dinner €20–€50.
closed	Never.
directions	On Vestibul, part of the Diocletian's Palace in the town centre.

	Vladimir Smoje
tel	+385 (0)21 329 329
fax	+385 (0)21 329 333
email	info@vestibulpalace.com
web	www.vestibulpalace.com

Hotel

Map 7 Entry 88

Hotel Peristil

Poljana Kraljica Jelene 5, Split, 21000 Split-Dalmatia

A modern hotel in a historic spot, Hotel Peristil rubs shoulders with the ancient masonry of Split's Old Town. On all sides are towering stone arches and the bases of vanished columns, some going back 1,700 years. The hotel is squeezed between the city cathedral and Split's crowning glory, the Diocletian's Palace. Although shiny and square from the outside, it has been thoroughly renovated inside – absolutely no trace of its past life as a rest home for partisans in the communist era. Rooms have wooden furniture, champagne-coloured bedcovers, ruffled muslin, round rugs, framed prints and the odd, friendly ornament. Two look onto the cathedral and the square behind that give the hotel its name. On the top floor, a plain white terrace offers grand rooftop views; downstairs a taverna, with tables on the square and a Dalmatian band playing in the evenings. Staff run things with a friendly professionalism and the food is well-regarded. A good choice for those looking for somewhere in the thick of things, but still quiet – except, of course, when the cathedral bells ring for the Sunday service.

Hotel

rooms	12 doubles.
price	€90–€120.
meals	Lunch & dinner €18.
closed	Never.
directions	Between cathedral & eastern (E) entrance (Silver Doors) to Diocletian's Palace, almost opposite Tourist Office.

	Daliborka Korptla
tel	+385 (0)21 329 070
fax	+385 (0)21 329 088
email	hotel.peristil@email.t-com.hr
web	www.hotelperistil.com

Map 7 Entry 89

Villa Rumba

Don Petra Cara 137, Gornja Podstrana, Podstrana, 21312 Split-Dalmatia

While beaches bake, you bask in breezes on the slopes above Podstrana. From up here, the Adriatic stretches west like turquoise silk, sprinkled with islands. Villa Rumba is actually two villas, one angular, modernist, icing-white, the other traditional, higher up the hill and stone-clad. Both are typically Mediterranean, both new, both hugely comfortable. The apartments are stylish and pleasing, their tiled and wooden floors cool underfoot, their furniture and fabrics vibrantly coloured, with the most characterful spaces those in the traditional house under the rafters. Manager Neven Banić lives on site and works to keep everything ticking over beautifully. You are surrounded by trim lawns, an amazing pool (artificial waves, laser lights) and an outdoor jacuzzi; it's a safe outdoor space that would be great for anyone with children. Cook in or out – there's a rustic summer kitchen – or treat yourself to Neven's local dishes in the restaurant. Come for the coast without the crush – and for historic Split, a 15-minute drive away. *Minimum stay seven nights. Bikes available for hire.*

rooms	7 apartments: 3 for 4-6, 4 for 2-4.
price	€120–€150 per night.
meals	Breakfast €5. Lunch & dinner €20-€30, by arrangment.
closed	Never.
directions	Follow coastal road south of Split for 8km. Podstrana is a series of hotels along the beach; Villa Rumba is signed to the left; 2km, on right.

Neven Banić

tel	+385 (0)21 332 109
mobile	+385 (0)91 204 8958
fax	+385 (0)21 332 104
email	info@villa-rumba.com
web	www.villa-rumba.com

Hotel & Self-catering

Map 7 Entry 90

Limunovo Drvo

Bunta, Sutivan, Brač Island, 21403 Split-Dalmatia

Named after the scented lemon tree in the front courtyard, Limunovo Drvo is every bit the Mediterranean summer house. It sits in the old part of Sutivan, a relaxing sprawl of stone houses and white pebble beaches with a small marina. Most visitors dash off to the south coast of the island leaving cobbled, arched Sutivan alone – a sweet, sleepy Adriatic village where donkeys carry farm produce and fishing boats bob. Limunovo Drvo's three floors are styled with a simple, modern elegance by English owners Jon and Penny Williams. Colours fit perfectly with the mood of the surroundings – brilliant whites, creamy wooden furniture, and cushions and sofas in pebble browns and greys. Most of the year the house is looked after by a local property agency; the interiors are spotless and the bed linen crisp. You can rent the whole house, or just part – the roomy, two-bedroom apartment upstairs or the smaller ground floor studio. Both have a kitchen and bathroom, plus plenty of comforting, homespun charm. *Minimum stay seven nights.*

Self-catering

rooms	House for 5 (1 apt for 3; 1 studio for 2). Extra sofabeds.
price	£300–£550 per week.
meals	Self-catering. Restaurants 200m.
closed	Never.
directions	Two-minute walk from Sutivan harbour. Ask for directions on booking.

	Penny Williams
tel	+44 (0)1225 865 591
email	willjo2000@hotmail.com
web	www.croatiancottage.co.uk

Map 7 Entry 91

Villa Adriatica

Put Vele Luke 31, Supetar, Brač Island, 21400 Split-Dalmatia

Zlatan and Nevenka Jelovac brought their knowledge and love of travel to this relaxed bolthole on Brač. Nevenka was born in Chile, Zlatan worked in the travel industry in America; expect a big welcome. Their small hotel in the coastal resort of Supetar may be modest in appearance but is known for its hospitality and its cultural events, including Croatian musical performances in summer. The Jelovacs' zest for life is reflected in their décor. Bedrooms are enlivened with dashes of colour, sea- and sand-themed paintings and sculptures create an aquatic mood, and the bric-a-brac that is dotted around came from an atelier in Split. Balconies catch the sunshine and some of Brač's best beaches are minutes away. The family know the island's secrets, its walking trails and hidden coves; follow the coastal path to Blaca Hermitage, perched in rocky country above sand-circled Blaca cove. The languorous pool and garden terrace are delightful, and protected from prying eyes by a screen of palms. *Minimum stay four nights July/August. Bikes available for hire.*

rooms	22: 11 doubles, 11 twins. Extra pull-out beds.
price	€79–€134. Half-board €109–€164 for 2.
meals	Breakfast not included. Dinner €15 (June-August).
closed	November-March.
directions	10-minute walk from Supetar port. Directions on booking.

	Zlatan Jelovac	Hotel
tel	+385 (0)21 343 806	
mobile	+385 (0)98 215 777	
fax	+385 (0)21 755 015	
email	info@villaadriatica.com	
web	www.villaadriatica.com	

Map 7 Entry 92

Palača Dešković
Pučišća, Brač Island, 21412 Split-Dalmatia

The Dešković family have lived in this robust, fortified mansion since the 15th century; staying here could be likened to staying in a French château or an English stately home. The Countess returned to her ancestral seat in 2004, and has revived its Renaissance grandeur. Moss was painstakingly brushed from the white stone walls and the rooms filled with the graceful lines of period furniture. Enter a world of carved bedsteads, glistening chandeliers and upholstered chaises longues – more Louis XVI than 21st-century Dalmatia. A few ultra-modern details have slipped through – in-room internet, air conditioning, hydromassage – while art courses and studio space for aspiring artists are in the offing. Ružica is a charming and easy-going hostess whose family history is a story in itself. The daughter of a Croatian count, she was raised in Zagreb by an Italian mother and her connections to Brač go back to the founding of Pučišća in the 15th century. It is one of the most historic settlements on the island, and dominated by a string of forts created by the island's celebrated stonemasons.

rooms	15: 7 twins, 8 suites.
price	€124–€206. Singles €93–€154. Suites €120–€248.
meals	Lunch & dinner €30.
closed	January–mid-February.
directions	From main square in Pučišća, towards church. Palača is next to it, clearly signed.

Hotel

	Ružica c-ssa Dešković
tel	+385 (0)21 788 240
mobile	+385 (0)98 209 718
fax	+385 (0)21 778 256
email	h.palaca-deskovic@st.t-com.hr
web	www.palaca-deskovic.com

Map 7 Entry 93

Villa Nena

Tina Ujevića 8, Bol, Brač Island, 21420 Split-Dalmatia

The terraces catch the famous breezes that make Bol a hot spot for wind- and kite-surfers. The villa was built from scratch by the owners on their favourite stretch of the Dalmatian coast – the south shore of Brač Island, with its hidden beaches, mountain monasteries and rugged coves. A simple exterior masks a stylish, imaginative and comfortable interior. Each of the self-catering apartments has a primary colour scheme that runs from bathrooms to bedspreads; the darker shades create a mood of cool sophistication, the pink and yellow apartments are bright and exuberant and much use is made of unusual fabrics. The front terraces are vast, their views stretching beyond the church and down to the sea. You may sample homemade wine and olive oil here, as well as fresh vegetables grown in the lovely villa gardens. The setting is well-nigh perfect – minutes from the beach, a short walk from Bol's marina and close to the start of the rough hiking trail to the cliffs at Blaca Hermitage. Come in June, when Bol opens up to the exciting windsurfing championships.

rooms	6 apartments: 2 for 2, 1 for 3, 1 for 4, 2 for 5. Also 2 studios for 2-4.
price	€35–€100. Studios €35–€62.
meals	Self-catering. Restaurants within a 10-minute walk.
closed	Never.
directions	10-minute walk northeast of Bol town centre. Directions on booking.

Self-catering

	Nena Marinković
tel	+385 (0)21 635 257
fax	+385 (0)21 635 849
email	nena.marinkovic@st.t-com.hr
web	www.er-corp.com/villanena

Map 7 Entry 94

Hotel Kaštil

Frane Radica 1, Bol, 21420 Split-Dalmatia

If you were to drop a silk scarf from your window it would sail across the Adriatic. Once a Turkish fortress, now an elegant small hotel, Kaštil overlooks a miniature marina in Bol's stone and terracotta Old Town, five minutes from a shingle beach. Behind, cobbled streets rise before rocky hills. In front, boats bob, seagulls wheel and holiday makers stroll along the promenade. The façade is all straight lines and cut stone; a fabulous terrace, shaded by columns and timber slats, looks out to sea. Inside, rough stone walls open to thoroughly modern spaces, decorated with the paintings and prints of artist Miljenko Romić. Bedrooms are understated not luxurious and every comfort is there, from air conditioning to double glazing. Beds are firm, pillows are plump and staff provide big hotel service at small hotel prices. To the side is a tree-shaded pizzeria recalling the Venetian history of Dalmatia, and a Balinese-themed cocktail bar with wicker chairs and straw parasols. For breakfast or afternoon tea there's one place to be – the front terrace, watching the boats and people come and go.

Hotel

rooms	32: 28 doubles, 4 triples.
price	€64–€140. Singles €44–€96. Triples €81–€159.
meals	Dinner, with wine, from 200 Kn.
closed	November-March.
directions	In the pedestrianised town centre. Directions on booking.

Renata Barać

tel	+385 (0)21 635 995
fax	+385 (0)21 635 997
email	kastil@kastil.hr
web	www.kastil.hr

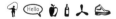

Map 7 Entry 95

Palmižana Meneghello
Palmižana Island, 21450 Split-Dalmatia

Imagine owning your own private bay facing the South Adriatic. This is the enviable position of Dagmar Meneghello, whose family founded Croatia's oldest herbal remedy company; Meneghello essential oils are still a standby of most medicine cabinets in Croatia. Luckily for visitors, Dagmar decided to share her island idyll. Now the bay is ringed by a pretty collection of villas, studios and apartments, set around two restaurants and a sand and pebble beach that gives way to waters as blue as Turkish glass. Natural stone walls conceal bright, contemporary living spaces full of lovely materials and radiant colours. Interiors also benefit from a rotating exhibition of Dagmar's collection of modern Croatian art. Alongside the fun and the modernity is Nature – cacti, mimosas, eucalyptuses, laurels, olives and aromatic herbs fill the grounds and assault the senses. In season, flowering rosemary scents the entire island. Out of season, the family organises a range of creative activities – art and cookery classes, wine tasting – for six or more interested guests. *Minimum stay seven nights.*

rooms	Villas: 2 for 4, 1 for 5, 1 for 6, 1 for 4. Studios: 3 for 3, 2 for 4. Apartments: 3 for 2, 3 for 4.
price	Villas €100–€420. Studios €80–€190. Apts €50–€200. Half-board extra €30–€35 p.p.
meals	Breakfast €10. Lunch & dinner €30–€50.
closed	December-March.
directions	From Hvar Town, water taxi to Palmižana. Signed from jetty (5-minute walk).

Hotel

	Tarin Meneghello
tel	+385 (0)21 717 270
mobile	+385 (0)91 478 3110
fax	+385 (0)21 717 268
email	tarin@palmizana.hr
web	www.palmizana.hr

Map 7 Entry 96

Villa Darinka

Vrboska, Hvar Island, 21463 Split-Dalmatia

Vrboska is a fishing town first and a yachting centre second. Hugging the shore at the end of a long narrow inlet crossed by a series of neat stone bridges, the town is picturesquely Mediterranean: narrow streets of stone houses, a quayside lined with fishing boats, vineyards behind. Set on the quieter northern shore, Villa Darinka is one of those peaceful family-run places to which the faithful return. It is a modern Croatian home inside and out, and its guest bedrooms are divided between two buildings. A third house has a guest living room with an open fire – a cosy haven for a cooler day. Owner Tonči Keršič runs the local tourist office so make the most of him; he is passionate about the area. Dinners are a mix of Croatian dishes and more familiar international staples, and bedrooms are simple but comfortable – wooden floors, wooden furniture, white walls, and a terrace for each. There's a cute little garden too, with fine views over the town and harbour. With three self-catering apartments, this is perfect for families – and for everyone seeking peace and sea air. *Bikes available for hire.*

Guest house & Self-catering

rooms	7 + 3: 7 doubles.
	3 apartments: 1 for 2, 2 for 4.
price	€17–€25. Apt for 2, €50–€70.
	Apt for 4, €80–€120.
meals	Breakfast €6. Dinner €12.
closed	November-March.
directions	From Vrboska harbour, follow quay round to far end. Over small bridge and along the opposite side of the bay. Villa Darinka is on left.

Tonči Keršić

tel	+385 (0)21 774 188
mobile	+385 (0)91 516 9351
fax	+385 (0)21 774 188

Map 7 Entry 97

Hotel Croatia

Majerovića bb, Hvar Town, Hvar Island, 21450 Split-Dalmatia

Much old-world elegance here, on the radiant island of Hvar. Officially the sunniest spot in Europe, Hotel Croatia is one of its finest assets; in a grove of pine trees and palms above a rocky shore, the hotel is a gleaming white beacon to boats out in the bay. Walking around the well-tended grounds, you half expect to bump into a character from a Scott Fitzgerald novel. Rooms have wrought-iron balconies facing the sea; wide stairways lead down through the gardens to the shore. Only party-goers flaunting champagne flutes are needed to complete the picture. The parkland setting brings other benefits: privacy and silence. No major roads pass by and chic Hvar Town is a ten-minute walk along the shore. Despite the classy feel, the welcome is agreeably down to earth; staff are courteous but friendly, leaving one relaxed not intimidated. Floating muslin and splashes of natural light soften the minimalist, slightly Puritan styling of the rooms. But they are lovely, with beautifully crafted wooden furniture and elegant, rose-tinted bathrooms. *Supplement charged for summer stays of under three nights.*

rooms	28: 22 doubles, 6 family rooms for 4.
price	€80–€160. Half-board €90–€200.
meals	Breakfast 50 Kn. Dinner 80 Kn.
closed	October-April.
directions	10-minute walk west of Hvar Town centre.

	Katica Čuljak
tel	+385 (0)21 742 400
fax	+385 (0)21 741 707
email	croatia-hvar@st.htnet.hr
web	www.hotelcroatia.net

Hotel

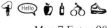

Map 7 Entry 98

Hotel Riva

Riva bb, Hvar Town, Hvar Island, 21450 Split-Dalmatia

Guarded by palm trees, lulled by the rigging of the marina's yachts, Hotel Riva stands a class apart. A refurbishment of a protected wharfside building, this smart design hotel is all cut stone and shuttered windows – a wonderfully sympathetic renovation for the old stone waterfront. Come evening, the façade glows orange in the sunset, and the fashionable seafood restaurants facing the marina are a stroll away. Behind the historic façade is a thoroughly modern hotel, designed with verve and kitted from floor to ceiling with boutique touches. Bathrooms shimmer with glass, chrome and mosaic. Bedrooms are dominated by black and white portraits of movie stars – James Dean, Brigitte Bardot, Audrey Hepburn; take your pick. The architects made the best possible use of the available space and the colours are subtle and contemporary. Well-trained staff are courteous and attentive – all that a landlocked yachtsman might wish for. For lesser mortals, smaller vessels from Korčula and Split moor just yards from the hotel.

rooms	54: 45 doubles, 1 twin, 8 suites.
price	€150-€300. Suites €200-€600.
meals	Lunch & dinner €8–€150.
closed	Never.
directions	From Sv Stjepana Square, west to the harbour, then south along quay to hotel.

Hotel

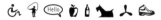

	Josip Čulić
tel	+385 (0)21 750 750
fax	+385 (0)21 750 751
email	reservations@suncanihvar.com
web	www.suncanihvar.com/riva

Map 7 Entry 99

stonehouse

Mudri Dolac, Hvar Island, 21465 Split-Dalmatia

Surrounded by olive groves, fields and vineyards is this immaculate conversion of traditional stone farm buildings outside Jelsa. It was a summer project that became a full-time occupation for ex-Londoner Neil Lewis, who fell in love with the site in 2003. The results are amazing. Hotel rooms are spread over the main farmhouse and several outbuildings, and the grounds are landscaped with boulders and streams. Simple whitewashed plaster, wood and local stone inform the interiors, with luxurious touches added. The open-plan bathrooms are particularly gorgeous, their naturally rounded blocks of stone serving as benches and partitions. Outside are a jacuzzi and an infinity pool, its waters cleansed by ozone not chlorine. In July and August, all ten bedrooms, sitting room and breakfast terrace are rented out as one. And you will be truly spoiled; a little boat ferries you to your own island beach; chefs are on hand to cook whatever you desire. A consecrated chapel makes this a pretty fine spot for weddings. All in all, stunning – with a price tag to match. *Minimum stay three to seven nights.*

rooms	10: 8 doubles, 2 family.
price	€300–€375. Half-board extra €30–€40 p.p. Whole house €30,000 per week.
meals	Catered house July/August. B&B rest of year.
closed	January-February.
directions	6km from Jelsa & Starigrad. Directions on booking.

	Neil Lewis
mobile	+385 (0)98 443 724
email	info@stonehousehvar.com
web	www.stonehousehvar.com

Hotel & catered house

Map 7 Entry 100

Pansion Murvica
Jelsa, Hvar Island, 21465 Split-Dalmatia

Đordan and Angelika met in Jelsa while he was a waiter and she was on holiday. The result? This charming small pension just outside the centre of Jelsa, its foliage-rich terrace restaurant fronting green fields and hills. The location is enchanting: Jelsa is dominated by a horseshoe-shaped harbour and the needle-like spire of the church of Sv Marija, while, over on the either side, forested coves promise peace and seclusion. The interiors here are modern but have the feel of home. They are airy, well-lit, uncluttered and painted in fresh colours, with well-equipped kitchenettes and soft towels in white bathrooms. The welcome is warm and genuine; Đordan and Angelika get along with everyone, from first-time travellers to mature globe-trotters, and foodies do particularly well. Đordan's family own plots of land all around Jelsa, and their organically-grown vegetables, wine and olive oil have been voted the best in Croatia for the past five years. All the ingredients in the restaurant are seasonal and perfectly fresh – including the fish straight from the bay. *Minimum stay seven nights July/August.*

Self-catering

rooms	7 apartments: 3 for 3, 1 for 4, 1 for 6.
price	€48–€132 per night. Half-board extra €20–€22 p.p.
meals	Breakfast €6. Lunch & dinner €14–€26.
closed	Restaurant closed November-Easter.
directions	5-minute walk from the centre of Jelsa. Detailed directions on booking.

	Angelika Gurdulić
tel	+385 (0)21 761 405
fax	+385 (0)21 761 405
email	info@murvica.net
web	www.murvica.net

Map 7 Entry 101

Humac House

Humac, Hvar Island, 21465 Split-Dalmatia

Restoring this tumble-down farmers' cottage was a labour of love for the Gurdulićs (who live at Pansion Murvica: see entry 101). In the family for generations, it now stands in original 17th-century glory. Đordan and Angelika plan eventually to retire here; for now, the house is rented out as a secluded country retreat. Very secluded, stunningly peaceful: the rest of the village is deserted. Don't expect towelling robes, bath salts or anything posh: the cottage is rustic and homely, its big, open-plan ground floor sharing a bedroom, a kitchen and a traditional open fire. Upstairs is a double mattress in the loft, ideal for children. You have the entire village to yourselves so don't feel shy about the open-air shower – it faces the ocean and distant Croatia. During the day, wander through the grapevines and olive groves; at night, relax with a glass of wine on the big front terrace serenaded by cicadas. This is as close as you can get to Croatian country living without picking the grapes yourself. And there's a simple country restaurant ten minutes away. *Minimum stay seven nights.*

rooms	Cottage for 2-4.
price	€400 per week.
meals	Self-catering. Restaurant 1km.
closed	Never.
directions	From Jelsa, 10km east (30-minute drive). Detailed directions on booking.

	Angelika Gurdulić
tel	+385 (0)21 761 405
fax	+385 (0)21 761 405
email	info@murvica.net
web	www.murvica.net

Self-catering

Map 7 Entry 102

Villa Nonna

Ribarska 50, Komiža, Vis Island, 21485 Split-Dalmatia

A tall townhouse on a narrow street in Vis's second city. Shuttered windows and a curvaceous wrought-iron balcony conceal seven exquisitely designed studios. The term 'studio' is misleading: here it is synonomous with space. Along with beautiful furniture, dark polished floorboards, immaculately renovated stone and alabaster-white walls. Shower rooms are smart, kitchenettes well-equipped, two apartments have cute Mediterranean balconies, another a tiny garden and all are filled with light. Only one studio has a separate living room but judicious use of space makes Villa Nonna feel larger than it really is. Another luxury: they store sufficient water to avoid rationing – often a problem on this small, dry island. Less well-known than Hvar or Korčula, Vis is nevertheless your classic Dalmatian island, all sandy coves, stone villages, Venetian ports and hills cloaked in vines. Once the villa was a taverna where diners cooked for themselves; today they arrange diving trips and cruises for you on a private yacht, the *Boston Whaler*. Perfect. *Minimum stay seven nights July/August.*

Self-catering

rooms	7 apartments for 2-3.
price	€50 per night.
meals	Self-catering. Restaurants 50m.
closed	Never.
directions	Walk to end of promenade, with sea on left. Pass Café Speed; 1st left; apartments 50m ahead.

Dražen Mikulčić
mobile	+385 (0)98 380 046
fax	+385 (0)1 463 6073
email	info@villa-nonna.com
web	www.villa-nonna.com

Map 7 Entry 103

Old Stone House

Rukavac b.b., Vis Island, 21480 Split-Dalmatia

The house was built from local stone by two brothers in the 1900s and was a meeting place for the Resistance during the German occupation of World War II. Vis, 17km by 8km, is one of the smaller islands in the Korčula-Hvar group, and is particularly charming. Vineyards criss-cross the slopes and the coast is ringed by beaches, crags and caves that are a dream for active folk. A few years ago the cottage was bought by an enterprising pair from Pembrokeshire, Wales, who transformed the rustic little place into an understatedly stylish home, with three guest bedrooms, living room and chill-out space in the loft. Vaulted wooden ceilings painted white create cool spaces above, rugs cover wooden floors and the views from the roof terrace are sublime. Craig and Xania also have several years' experience teaching physical education between them and can arrange whatever activities you want, from sea-kayaking, snorkelling and mountain biking to yoga and boules. Rooms are rented by the week and include a six-day activity programme. The food sounds fabulous. *Minimum stay seven nights. Bikes available for hire.*

rooms	3: 2 doubles, 1 family room for 4.
price	€1,600–€1,900 per week. Includes 5 lunches, 3 dinners & 6 days of activities.
meals	Part half-board. Restaurants 200m.
closed	November-May.
directions	Transfer from Vis town ferry included.

	Craig & Xania Wear
tel	+44 (0)1834 814533
mobile	+385 (0)98 131 4179
email	info@wearactive.com
web	www.wearactive.com

Guest house

Map 7 Entry 104

South Dalmatia: Croatia's First Lady

When travellers think of Croatia they think of Southern Dalmatia. A string of idyllic islands and shingle and sand beaches, this is the Mediterranean as it used to be. All along the coast are the unmistakable relics of the Venetian empire: mighty fortified cities guarding harbours and inlets. The atmosphere is unexpectedly Italian, and it is the hottest part of the country.

The undisputed capital of the southern Dalmatia coast is Dubrovnik – a magnificent medieval port shielded by mighty Venetian walls. Its stunning gothic architecture and fortress grandeur attract holiday makers by day; at night the mood changes, as tavernas and 'hole-in-the-wall' bars fill with locals and those who have chosen to stay within the old city walls. The Old Town is protected as a UNESCO World Heritage Site; the UN has cleared away all traces of the Yugoslav War and the streets gleam. A network of ferry routes fans out from Dubrovnik to most of the Dalmatian islands, making the city a superb base for island-hopping adventures.

Beyond the Old Town is the sprawling new town, extending north along the coast and west onto the Lapad peninsula. This is where most of Dubrovnik's inhabitants live, and where you find the tourists after hours. Nearby Zaton Bay is a tranquil beach spot where the wealthy once built their summer houses. Many holiday makers choose to stay in Cavtat, a pretty beach-fringed port 12 miles south.

Just west of Dubrovnik, the island of Mljet is a botanist's dream and the only place in Europe with wild mongooses (originally introduced to rid the island of its snakes). A third of the island is preserved as a national park, shielding rich wildlife and preserved monasteries that go back to the Middle Ages.

Further north, the beautiful Pelješac Peninsula is home to the vineyards that produce some of Croatia's best-known wines. The tradition of winemaking dates back to Roman times, when Pelješac wines were the lubricant for extravagant feasts of oysters and mussels. The waters of Mali Ston Bay still produce the best oysters in Croatia, if not Europe.

Croatians claim that Marco Polo was born in Korčula, the capital of the island of the same name. The popular Old Town is squeezed onto a thumb-shaped isthmus projecting into the bay, and is a charming tangle of narrow stone lanes. The rest of the island is famous for its fine beaches, translucent waters and Greek and Roman remains – a verdant paradise where the smell of pine mingles with the scent of the sea.

Photo Kathryn Tomasetti

South Dalmatia

Pločica Lighthouse
Pločica Island, Dubrovnik-Neretva

It takes a rare degree of commitment to fulfil a childhood dream; Ante Petković did just that when he took over the lighthouse on Pločica – his piece of paradise. The island measures 800 by 300 metres, a lovely, lonely wedge of stone emerging from the blue Adriatic, midway between Korčula and Hvar. On one shore, the land dips into the water creating a perfect current-free beach. On the other, a rocky wall rises to the foot of the lighthouse, a perfectly proportioned structure built in 1887. Up to 14 people can stay, in two simply styled apartments with plenty of bathrooms – but you are asked to use water and electricity with discretion! As you rest on the terrace, the eye is drawn to the open ocean. At night, you will spot the twinkle of other lighthouses along the Korčulanski channel. Guests are mostly happy to cook – don't forget the provisions – but Ante can also ferry you over to a couple of small tavernas on the island of Šćedro. Enjoy the safe beach for children, fishing at dawn on the south and west coasts, panoramic views and perfect peace. *Minimum stay seven nights in summer. No heating.*

Lighthouse

rooms	2 apartments: 1 for 6, 1 for 8.
price	€573–€1,149 per week.
meals	Self-catering. Provisons available at extra charge. Lunch & dinner on request. Shops on nearby island.
closed	Never.
directions	Ferry to Korčula; lighthouse keeper can collect (extra charge). Or transfer from Prigradica on Pločica by dinghy (15 mins/€120).

	Adriatica.net
tel	+44 (0)20 7183 0437
fax	+385 (0)1 245 2909
email	info@adriatica.net
web	www.adriatica.net

Map 7 Entry 105

Villa Mediterane
Viganj 224, Kućište, 20267 Dubrovnik-Neretva

Fishermen's houses line the harbour wall of the sleepy resort of Orebić, and the streets are dotted with cypresses and pines. A string of foliage-backed beaches stretches northwest to Viganj – and the Villa Mediterane sitting unobtrusively on the shore. Palms and pines part to reveal a gleaming white, modernist exterior, plus two swimming pools circled by sun umbrellas and recliners. Windsurfers play off the hotel beach, exploiting the Maestral winds; the less energetic are to be found dipping their toes in the surf. Rooms have been styled with an unexpected spontaneity, their wooden floors and painted wooden furniture creating the feel of a Key West hotel. Delightful staff devote themselves to looking after you, and this is a great place for families, with several self-catering apartments and plenty of safe spots outdoors. Meals promise local ingredients and Croatian wines: reds from Orebić, whites from across the channel in Korčula. It's a marvellous little place and with a car you can explore all those fishing villages along the Pelješac peninsula. *Minimum stay three nights July/August. Bikes available for hire.*

rooms	12 + 11: 12 doubles. 11 apartments for 2-4.
price	€40-€70. Singles less 20%. Half-board €30–€45 p.p. Apartments €40–€85. Prices per night.
meals	Dinner €13.
closed	November-March.
directions	From Orebić, 8km northwest along coast. Detailed directions on booking.

Hotel & Self-catering

	Tomislav Ančić
tel	+385 (0)20 719 096
mobile	+385 (0)91 615 5003
fax	+385 (0)20 719 106
email	korcula-bus@du.htnet.hr
web	www.villa-mediterane.com

Map 7 Entry 106

Slaven Apartments

Čara, Zavalatica, Korčula Island, 20273 Dubrovnik-Neretva

Zavalatica is as quiet as anything out of season; in summer, it bursts into village-festival life. The southern half of Korčula Island is more rural and Croatian in feel than the north and the countryside around Zavalatica is full of fascinating small villages: Čara, famous for its wines, and Čavića luka, famous for the miraculous appearance of the Madonna in 1686. Zavalatica itself is a pretty seaside town emerging from a forested valley, its wedge-shaped stone harbour lined with fishermen's cottages. Reached by a vine-covered stairway above the harbour, these apartments are homely, spotless and accessible. Maintained with care by Slaven and other members of the Laus family, each has a kitchen/dining room, two bathrooms, two bedrooms and a terrace leading off the main bedroom, with views over the village and coast. Staying here is a bit like staying with kindly grandparents – you may well be plied with the wine, olive oil and vegetables that the couple grow on their plot outside the village, and may even be invited to help out come harvest time!

Self-catering

rooms	2 apartments for 4.
price	€40–€55.
meals	Self-catering. Restaurant 50m.
closed	Never.
directions	Split-Vela Luka ferry; road to Blato & Smokvice; 2km to Zavalatica harbour. Westwards, road curves up out of town; apartments on left. Call ahead to be met as tricky to find.

Slaven Laus

tel	+385 (0)20 834 036
mobile	+385 (0)91 783 8340

Map 8 Entry 107

Roberta's Guesthouse
Put Sv Nikole 24, Korčula Town, Korčula Island, 20260 Dubrovnik-Neretva

Roberta inherited this charming townhouse from her grandmother, who ran it as a B&B when visitors to Korčula were Croatian. The clientele may have changed, but the welcome is equally whole-hearted. She runs the place with effusive efficiency – guests have compared the experience to visiting their own grandmother's house as children. Rooms wrap you up in old-fashioned comfort, communal spaces are full of family heirlooms and window sills and terrace spill over with flowers. The house is just minutes from the ferry stop in Korčula and its windows look onto the sea and harbour and the terracotta-tiled houses of the old town. The guest house is traditional but not austere, with its white walls and interesting hand-crafted furniture. The rooms at the front are our favourites: one has a sea-facing terrace, the other has unusual picture windows that allow you to watch the harbour and its bobbing boats from the comfort of your bed. The shared bathrooms may not appeal to everyone, but the position and the tradition make this an enchanting place to stay.

rooms	4: 2 doubles, 2 triples, sharing two bathrooms.
price	180 Kn-240 Kn. Singles 90 Kn-150 Kn. Triples 180 Kn-330 Kn.
meals	Restaurants 200m.
closed	Never.
directions	From Korčula jetty, walk west to Pomerinja Square, then south into Put Sv Nikole.

Guest house

	Roberta Maričić-Kondenar
tel	+385 (0)20 711 247
mobile	+385 (0)91 799 5728
email	robertamk@hotmail.com

Map 8 Entry 108

Tarle Family's Apartments & Rooms

Šetalište Frana Kršinića, Korčula Town, Korčula Island, 20260 Dubrovnik-Neretva

You could say the Tarle brothers have the best of both worlds: the laid-back lifestyle of Korčula in the summer, and the beaches and blue skies of Australia in the winter. When the brothers have flown, their mother provides the welcome at this character-filled guest house on the outskirts of the Old Town, assisted by a coterie of local ladies. Mediterranean mothers have a reputation for well-intentioned fussing, so don't be surprised if you are plied with biscuits and smiles. Along the driveway bees buzz around the flowers and trailing vines create a shady bower on either side. The décor harks back to the Croatia of the 1960s. Tiles are laid in patterns that will charm fans of post-modern design and each room is unique, with eclectic furniture and miniature balconies. The décor is dated, but in the most endearing manner. Rooms embrace a haven of a garden, with canopies of branches providing shade for reading and eating en plein air. Many guests cook meals out here, but the restaurants of old Korčula are a short walk away, down quiet residential streets.

Rooms & Self-catering

rooms	4 + 3: 4 doubles. 3 apartments: 1 for 2, 1 for 4, 1 for 5.
price	€29–€35. Apartments €65–€75.
meals	Breakfast not available. Restaurants 1km.
closed	Never.
directions	Follow signs from town dir. Lumbarda; at 1st major curve, see sign for Marko Polo Hotel; follow this turn-off; Tarle at end of road.

	Mario & Branco Tarle
tel	+385 (0)20 711 712 or +385 (0)20 834 036

Map 8 Entry 109

Family Ojdanić

Dinka Sarnećica-Nedana 1, Sv Nikole, Korčula Town, Korčula Island, 20260 Dubrovnik-Neretva

Roko Ojdanić is one of Korčula's characters. As well as being the owner of these very appealing apartments on the hillside above Korčula harbour, he runs a taxi service between the islands. (His destination signs read 'Orebić', 'Korčula' and 'Anywhere'.) The apartments stand in wonderful terraced gardens brimming with fruit trees, geraniums and roses. Bedrooms are fresh and airy, with simple furnishings, white walls and big picture windows framing views of Korčula Bay and the Old Town – a classic panorama of church spires, white stone walls and tawny rooftops. Roko has taken great care to entwine your terraces with grapevines, so you may dine alfresco, shaded from the midday sun. All is beautifully maintained, bathrooms are a decent size and kitchenettes are well-equipped. To top it all, you can take trips around the islands on Roko's boat, which is a bit like having your very own water chauffeur. The Old Town, famous for its cathedral and medieval buildings, is a short stroll downhill. *Bikes available for hire.*

rooms	2 apartments: 1 for 2, 1 for 2-4.
price	€80–€100 per night.
meals	Self-catering. Restaurants 200m.
closed	Never.
directions	5-minute walk uphill from Korčula's Old Town, harbour & bus station. Detailed directions on booking.

Self-catering

	Roko Ojdanić
tel	+385 (0)20 716 633
mobile	+385 (0)91 515 2555
fax	+385 (0)20 716 633
email	roko-taxi@du.t-com.hr

Map 8 Entry 110

Pansion Marinka

Lumbarda, Korčula Island, 20263 Dubrovnik-Neretva

Pansion Marinka is set in countryside draped with the vines that produce Croatia's famous grk wines. It is a deeply restorative place, and owners Frano and Višnja tend both grapes and guests effortlessly. She is a keen cook, he loves to share stories of growing up on a working farm in the days before modern machinery. (If you are interested in the history of the island, ask Frano; he will happily oblige.) The farmhouse itself is a typical modern Dalmatian home: roomy, comfortable, with a flower-spilled terrace and the odd resident goat. You'll see similar houses across the island, but few offer this level of hospitality. The best guest rooms sport mock-marble bathrooms and the rest have glazed tiles in colourful patterns on the floors and quirky décor. All are pleasing. The Bire family has farmed this area for over 600 years. As well as wine, the farm produces olive oil, fruit and vegetables; everything served in the small indoor restaurant has been organically grown. The countryside is gorgeous, but you'll need a car or scooter for sorties to the historic town of Lumbarda. *Longer stays preferred in summer.*

rooms	10 doubles.
price	€20–€30.
meals	Breakfast €5.
	Dinner, with wine, €10.
closed	Never.
directions	6km drive south of Korčula Town.
	Detailed directions on booking.

Restaurant with rooms

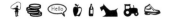

	Frano Milina Bire
tel	+385 (0)20 712 007
mobile	+385 (0)98 344 712
email	marinka.milina-bire@du.htnet.hr

Map 8 Entry 111

Juraj Kopac

OreBeach Club Hotel

Kralja Petra Krešimira 141, Orebić, 20250 Dubrovnik-Neretva

Cocooned by trees, dusted with sands, this club-hotel is bliss for seekers of sun, sand and surf: the channel between Orebić and Korčula Island is windsurfer heaven. Cooled by the shade of pines, maritime oaks and cypresses between Orebić and the windsurfing beach at Viganj, OreBeach also has a scuba club, for diving in the crystal waters of the Pelješki channel. If you prefer, just laze on the private beach – bliss with its ivory-coloured sands and clear blue waters. The hotel was built by a Dutch couple in 2002 and clean modern lines inform the décor. Bedrooms are large, light and decorated in crisp whites, accented by the beautiful tones of natural woods. It is all perfectly maintained. Bedrooms with front-facing balconies are a pebble's throw from the sea, and breakfasts are served on the terrace, accompanied by views of Korčula Island. When evening falls, linger over a long drink in the beach bar as the sun dips below the horizon. Orebić is a ten-minute stroll along the shore – unless you decide to zip off on your bike or scooter. *30% supplement for under three nights.*

rooms	17: 13 doubles, 3 triples, 1 family room for 4.
price	€50–€95. Half-board extra €12 p.p.
meals	Lunch & dinner 150 Kn-200 Kn.
closed	Never.
directions	From Orebić town centre, 1km west towards Viganj; hotel signed on right.

Croatian Tourist Board

Hotel

	Višnja Vukotić
tel	+385 (0)20 713 985
fax	+385 (0)20 713 986
email	kisik@du.htnet.hr
web	www.orebeachclubhotel.com

Map 8 Entry 112

Palagruža Lighthouse
Palagruža Island, Dubrovnik-Neretva

Crowning a rocky spur that runs along the spine of rugged Palagruža Island, the lighthouse has been guarding the channel between Croatia and Italy since 1875. No fair-weather lighthouse – Palagruža sits 65 nautical miles out in the Adriatic, accessible by fast motor launch from Korčula. Once the boat drops you off in the sheltered pebbled bay, a week lies ahead with only the seabirds and two lighthouse keepers for company. Towering 100m above the bay, there's a ropeway to transport bags and provisions and, at the base, two basic but comfortably furnished apartments. If you do tire of the 1,400m by 300m island, the lighthouse keepers can whisk you off to neighbouring isles – and mornings hauling in the nets with fishermen from the mainland. It is a setting for novelists and poets – Mediterranean scrub and wild capers cover the rocky hillsides, clear blue waters stretch to the horizon. Legend tells that Palagruža was the final resting place of Diomedes, hero of the Trojan wars. For the right kind of people, the privacy and sense of romance are unsurpassed. *Minimum stay seven nights.*

rooms	2 apartments for 4.
price	€819–€919 per week.
meals	Self-catering. Bring provisions. Lunch & dinner on request.
closed	October-May.
directions	Scheduled boat transfer from Korčula (2 hrs/€380).

Lighthouse

	Adriatica.net
tel	+44 (0)20 7183 0437
fax	+385 (0)1 245 2909
email	info@adriatica.net
web	www.adriatica.net

Map 8 Entry 113

Mrčara Island

Off Lastovo Island, Dubrovnik-Neretva

Mrčara is a place for Swiss Family Robinsons. More goats than people live on this lush green islet in the Adriatic, the Pavelins's wilderness home. Free spirits, the couple generate all their own electricity and wash and cook with natural rain water. Until 1979, the island belonged to the army, but the Pavelins took it on in 1999 and created this hideaway. Guests stay in basic bedrooms in the main house or in three wooden huts by the beach, each with a rudimentary shower. Interiors are as simple as they come – just a collection of beds that could almost have been brought here by the waves and a wooden roof overhead – but little tied curtains add homely touches and fishing nets, broken amphorae and pieces of flotsam and jetsam contribute to the laid-back mood. At the front is a pretty sand and pebble beach; the rest of the island has a rocky shoreline, brilliant for fishing and snorkelling. Inland, younger explorers can hunt for the giant 10 kilogram rabbit. Guests tend to be an interesting bunch, communal meals in the evenings promise lively conversation and the simple meals sound delicious.

rooms	9: 2 doubles, 1 triple, sharing 2 bathrooms; 3 huts for 4.
price	Half-board €60–€86. Triple €90–€129. Hut €120–€172.
meals	Half-board only.
closed	Never.
directions	Ferry Split-Ubli; Lastovo Island 50nm/92km. From there, owners pick up.

	Branko & Rada Pavelin
tel	+385 (0)99 212 0853
mobile	+385 (0)21 384 279
email	branko.pavelin@st.t-com.hr
web	www.adriatic-lastovo.vze.com

Guest house

Map 8 Entry 114

Struga Lighthouse

Skrivena luka 110, Lastovo Island, 20290 Dubrovnik-Neretva

Lastovo stands out amongst the Dalmatian islands for its wild terrain – a series of rounded bluffs and hills sparsely covered by pine and maquis. Struga Lighthouse tops a sheer cliff on a rocky promontory on the south side; its lantern has protected ships since 1837. In the submerged caves below, lighthouse keepers once caught an 18kg lobster, so vast it was presented to the Austro-Hungarian emperor; you, too, may strike lucky. Although Struga doesn't quite match other Adriatic lighthouses for isolation, you do have a proper island to explore. There are small stone villages, untouched beaches and, unbelievably, a packed calendar of festivals; in one, a villager is somewhat alarmingly hurled down a cliff on a rope in commemoration of the thwarting of a Turkish invasion. Now the lighthouse contains four spartan apartments sleeping two to five, all looked after by the kindly Kvinta family who have tended the lighthouse for generations. Jure catches fish and picks up provisions from the nearest village, Rada cooks tasty meals for both family and guests. *Minimum stay three to seven nights.*

Lighthouse

rooms	4 apartments for 2-5.
price	€299–€949 per week.
meals	Self-catering. Provisions available at extra charge. Dinner €15–€20
closed	Never.
directions	Ferry (5 hours) from Split to Ubli on Lastovo. 20km gravel road to lighthouse. Transfer can be arranged.

	Adriatica.net
tel	+44 (0)20 7183 0437
fax	+385 (0)1 245 2909
email	info@adriatica.net
web	www.adriatica.net

Map 8 Entry 115

Villa Jezero

Njivice 2, Govedari, Mljet Island, 20226 Dubrovnik-Neretva

As far from the madding crowd as you can get. In the Mljet National Park, forested hills surround you and salt lakes reflect cloudless skies above. This was the island where Ulysses was charmed and captured by Calypso, so they say; even today, there's the feeling of enchantment. You arrive at the tiny jetty at Polače, where Ivan Stražičić waits to ferry new arrivals across the lake on his tiny boat. The only other way to get here is on foot – a serene stroll along the lakeshore past small beaches and crystal clear pools. In the villa are six comfortable suites, all with sitting rooms, done up in simple Mediterranean style with bright bedspreads, plain white walls and windows that lead the eye to the stunning views beyond. The family run the villa with the easy-going humour of those free of the stresses and strains of urban life. Meals are prepared in the family kitchen by the animated Nikola, Ivan's mother, using favourite family recipes. A place for lazy days on the beach and peaceful strolls around the lake. Or energetic forays via boat, kayak or bike. *Minimum stay two nights during high season.*

rooms	6 suites: 2 for 4, 3 for 3, 1 for 2.
price	€60–€100.
meals	Breakfast €8. Lunch & dinner €20.
closed	Never.
directions	By car from Pelješac peninsula take ferry from Prapratno harbour to Mljet. Also afternoon ferry from Dubrovnik. From Polače jetty, National Park bus (free if you are staying on Mljet) to owners' boat across lake (2 mins).

	Ivan Stražičić	Guest house
tel	+385 (0)20 744 019	
mobile	+385 (0)91 784 1655	
email	pansionjezero@net.hr	
web	www.jezero.tk	

Map 8 Entry 116

Apartment Tedo

Komarna b.b., Klek, 20356 Dubrovnik-Neretva

Visitors descend on the historic cities of Split, Trogir and Dubrovnik. Things are quieter here; Komarna is a summer village for Croatian city dwellers and overlooks the vine-covered spur of the Pelješac peninsula. There is no old town, just tidy modern houses and sand and pebble beaches tucked into a cypress-covered headland where families picnic and fishermen dry their nets. Here you have four neat apartments 40 metres from the water, so you can be out of your chair and in the sea in seconds. What marks Tedo out is the laid-back appoach of the owners; the garden used to have a vegetable patch but tortoises ate the produce so they got rid of the patch and kept the tortoises. (Children may feed them with permission!). Two or more families holidaying together get just the right balance of privacy and personal space, thanks to the safely enclosed garden by day and the shared barbecue terrace by night. Each apartment is identical, with kitchen, living room and terrace downstairs, and bathroom, bedrooms and balcony above. All are styled simply and well. *Minimum stay five nights.*

rooms	4 apartments for 4.
price	€50–€75 per night.
meals	Self-catering. Restaurants 200m.
closed	November–March.
directions	Off E65, 70km north of Dubrovnik. Komarna turning is between marker-boulders Km 733 & Km 734. Enter village, towards Villa Bili; apartments on left.

Self-catering

	Jan Skov
tel	+45 (0)4491 5940
mobile	+45 (0)2880 4693
fax	+45 (0)4491 5940
email	jan@komarna.com
web	www.komarna.com

Map 8 Entry 117

Family Daničić Guesthouse
Puhijera 4, Sudurad, Šipan Island, 20223 Dubrovnik-Neretva

Is it the sunshine or the vineyards laden with grapes that has earned Šipan the nickname 'Golden Island'? Perhaps it is the bounty of the sea: more than 70% of the fish sold in Dubrovnik's markets is caught in the deep channels surrounding Šipan. Whatever, this very untouristy island remains captivatingly peaceful and coated with a tapestry of vineyards, olive groves, stone churches and rusticity. Boats arrive at the tiny harbour of Sudurad; from here it's a short and gentle stroll though fields and olive groves to the Family Daničić Guesthouse. Surrounded by fruit trees and vegetable gardens, this is a small-scale, family B&B, run by Tonci and his mother, who are friendly but not intrusive. It's a new house built in the traditional style, with a sunny balcony upstairs and a shaded terrace below, and the décor is pure Croatian – white walls, flowing curtains, wooden furniture. The family produce their own olive oil and wine and you may pluck their fruits and vegetables to your heart's desire. An authentic slice of Croatian island life.
Minimum stay five nights June-September.

rooms	5 + 1: 3 doubles; 2 doubles sharing bath. 1 apartment for 2-4.
price	€30–€40. Singles €15–€20. Apartment €30–€40.
meals	Restaurants 200m.
closed	December-March.
directions	From jetty, walk through town's main square alongside water; follow pedestrianised road; 200m, on left.

Tonci Daničić

tel	+385 (0)20 758 166
mobile	+385 (0)91 518 7222 (reservations)
fax	+385 (0)20 486 065
email	toncidanicic@yahoo.com

Guest house & Self-catering

Map 8 Entry 118

La Villa

Obala Iva Kuljevana 33, Lopud Island, 20222 Dubrovnik-Neretva

Picture an island with empty beaches and ruins strewn across its hills. Imagine a 19th-century Renaissance-styled mansion, surrounded by ornamental gardens, where you step out of the front door and onto the sand. This is La Villa. The house was built in 1862 for the Baron of Mayneri. Now it is a sophisticated B&B, refined yet relaxed and even more elegant inside than out. Hosts Dobrila and Mischel invite you to enter a world where minimalist design rubs shoulders with classical style. White muslin curtains flutter in the breeze as guests recline in wave-shaped seats or wicker rocking chairs. Light and space are the key notes here and the meditative mood is complemented by crisp cotton sheets and white walls in beautifully serene rooms. The living room has a screen for films and a small internet 'station'; outside is a sun-dappled terrace, a boules court and a seating area beneath an ancient magnolia. The grounds lead directly into the lovely, shady Giorgi-Mayneri botanical park. Lush Lopud Island, an hour from Dubrovnik, feels like another world. *Minimum stay three nights July/August.*

rooms	6: 4 doubles, 1 family, 1 suite.
price	€70–€153. Singles €50–€135.
meals	Dinner on request. Restaurants 200m.
closed	November–March; Easter.
directions	From Lopud ferry, 400m west along seafront.

Guest house

	Dobrila Carić & Mischel Cuculić
tel	+385 (0)20 759 259
mobile	+385 (0)91 322 0126
fax	+385 (0)20 759 259
email	contact@lavilla.com.hr
web	www.lavilla.com.hr

Map 8 Entry 119

Villa Pepe

Potok 28, Trsteno, 20233 Dubrovnik-Neretva

Even the trees have a story to tell in Trsteno: the town arboretum was planted on the orders of a noble family, using seeds from far-off lands gathered by Venetian traders. Visitors are still humbled by the soaring oriental planes in the main square. The handsome modern Villa Pepe has a prime spot in this leafy settting, perched above the sea wall, surrounded by sprawling gardens of its own. On arrival, clamber a flight of steep steps to be rewarded by views of the ocean and the island of Šipan. Downstairs, guests have dining room, a floral sofa'd living room and a very well-equipped kitchen leading to a large terrace and pool. From here, a paved path takes you down to the rocky beach and crystal waters – bliss for swimming. Bedrooms are above the owners' self-contained level, on the top floor where the mood is opulent without being overly modern: bold colours, polished marble, gold taps, a jacuzzi… and views that will have you leaping out of bed in the morning. Owner Mandaljena Trojanović divides her time between tending her guests and her garden; flowers are her passion. *Minimum stay seven nights. Bikes available for hire.*

rooms	Villa for 6.
price	€2,800 per week.
meals	Self-catering.
	Restaurants in Trsteno, 2km.
closed	Never.
directions	From Dubrovnik, 15km north to Trsteno, then left at main square. Villa is past campsite, at end of steps.

	Mandaljena Trojanović	Self-catering
tel	+385 (0)20 751 093	
mobile	+385 (0)20 816 512	
email	i.p.trojanovic@du.htnet.hr	

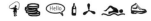

Map 8 Entry 120

Zaton Mali 108

Bulet 33, Zaton Mali, 20235 Dubrovnik-Neretva

Zaton, the summer retreat of Dubrovnik nobles, has long been a green escape from the city. The hamlet of Zaton Mali is the smaller cousin of Zaton Veliki: a cluster of stone houses on the hillside overlooking the bay. Set back from the water, Snježena's house – once an olive press – has wonderful views: its south-facing rooms take in the tree-fringed shoreline and the largest magnolia in Croatia. The guest apartment backs onto a pot-filled patio that leads to a large and lovely, tumbling garden where you wander among oranges and figs, kiwis and lemons. The renovation was a Herculean task for the energetic Snježena and she has created a light, colourful, open plan house which is both modern and homely. There are plants galore and attractive wooden furniture, some of which followed Snježena from Germany, some of which she has restored herself. She is aided by her daughter Rhubin – who you'll probably speak to when you book – and they make a happy team. Just in case life gets too peaceful, you are five miles from Dubrovnik's bright lights. *Minimum stay five nights in high season.*

Self-catering

rooms	Apartment for 6.
price	€100–€150.
meals	Self-catering. Restaurants 50m.
closed	November-April.
directions	North from Dubrovnik for Split, cross new bridge to Zaton Mali. Restaurant parking on right as you enter village.

	Rhubin Emanuella Herceg
tel	+385 (0)20 891 154
mobile	+385 (0)91 555 4003
email	zatonmali108@net.hr
web	www.dubrovnik-online.com/apartment_zatonmali/

Map 8 Entry 121

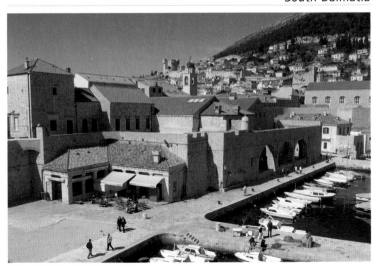

Karmen Apartments
Bandureva 1, Dubrovnik, 20000 Dubrovnik-Neretva

Is this the finest spot in old Dubrovnik's Venetian port? Fishermen unload hauls of glistening bream and lobster onto the stone quay; on the next cobbled street, the morning sun touches the Rector's Palace, grand with its Renaissance colonnade, and the baroque cathedral, Sicilian in its flamboyance. The van Bloemens arrived from London in 1972; Marc's parents founded the legendary Troubadour Coffee House where Jimi Hendrix played. The bohemian influence seems to have rubbed off here: these four apartments are refreshingly homely with a pretty mix of old and new furniture and homespun spreads – unusual in an area known for its antique-chic style. There are artistic touches – a painting here, fresh flowers there – while the windows frame vignettes of the UNESCO-protected old city. Three generations of the family live on the top two floors of this immaculate building and Marc is dedicated to keeping Dubrovnik beautiful: he it was who led the battle against brand-name parasols, now banned. Air-conditioning units and awnings are next. *Supplement charged for stays under three nights.*

rooms	4 apartments for 2-3.
price	€75–€120.
meals	Self-catering. Restaurants 100m.
closed	Never.
directions	With your back to the clock tower on Stradun, left, past cathedral, following signs for aquarium; Karmen Apartments signed in alley on left; 50m on right.

Self-catering

	Marc & Silva van Bloemen
tel	+385 (0)20 323 433
mobile	+385 (0)98 619 282
email	mvb@karmendu.tk
web	www.karmendu.com

Map 8 Entry 122

Apartments Amoret 1 & Amoret 2

Restićeva 2 & Dinka Ranjine 5, Dubrovnik, 20000 Dubrovnik-Neretva

The Amoret apartments are divided between two 500-year-old buildings in Dubrovnik's charming Old Town. Both buildings have been recently and sympathetically restored and the rooms filled with Secessionist furniture; the aristocratic former owners would surely have approved. The house on Dinka Ranjine Street is the grander property, with an old well in the entrance hall and a cellar room for breakfast. All the apartments are spacious and atmospheric – Revelin on the first floor is particularly appealing – with their nostalgic collection of wooden bedsteads and traditional Croatian adornments. The two ground-floor studios are also a particularly good find; self-catering places for the less sprightly or able are rare in the centre of the city. The apartments are near the Jesuit Monastery but on quietish streets; double-glazed windows keep out any city squawk. The icing on this particularly splendid cake comes in the form of Branka, a friendly and enthusiastic hostess. She enjoys practising her English and will go out of her way to ensure you have a happy stay.

rooms	8 apartments for 2. Additional beds.
price	€60–€120. Breakfast by arrangement, at extra cost.
meals	Self-catering. Restaurants 100m.
closed	Never.
directions	50m from Stradun, the Old Town's main thoroughfare. Detailed directions on booking.

Self-catering

	Branka & Ivica Dabrović
tel	+385 (0)20 324 005
mobile	+385 (0)91 530 4910
email	dubrovnik@post.t-com.hr
web	www.dubrovnik-amoret.com

Map 8 Entry 123

Apartments Toni
Ivana Zajca 5, Dubrovnik, 20000 Dubrovnik-Neretva

A spirit-lifting view greets visitors at Apartments Toni. Just metres from the sea, overlooking Gruž's harbour, the 100-year-old stone house caught Dubravka Tolja's eye in the 1990s. She promptly scooped it up and spent three years renovating from top to toe. Now she looks after guests with thoughtful charm and is more than happy to take you on trips up the down the coast – to Konavle, Cavtat, Trsteno Arboretum and Lokrum, with its secluded beaches. The apartments are in Lapad, just a ten-minute bus ride from the Old Town, next to the yacht club and Restaurant Orsant. Work up an appetite at the tennis club, or spend a few hours fishing from the rocks by way of a digestif. Downstairs are two studios; upstairs can be rented as separate rooms, or as an apartment for ten; at the very top are two bedrooms, bathrooms and jacuzzi. The style is flamboyant, slightly chintzy, with satin bedspreads, period furniture, feminine fuss. The house is often used for filming ads and magazine features; chaps arriving by yacht – we're sure you're out there – can use the Toljas' nearby mooring.

rooms	9: 5 doubles (or 1 apartment for 10); 2 doubles sharing bath (or 1 apartment for 4); 2 studios for 2.
price	€70. Studios €50. Apartment for 4, €120. Apartment for 10, €350.
meals	Self-catering. Restaurant next door.
closed	Never.
directions	Coming from Dubrovnik Old Town, head for yacht club & Restaurant Orsan; house next door.

Self-catering

	Dubravka Tolja
mobile	+385 (0)91 529 4741
email	dubravka.tolja@du.t-com.hr
web	www.apartmanitoni.com

Map 8 Entry 124

Karmen's House

Ivana Rabljanina 7, Dubrovnik, 20000 Dubrovnik-Neretva

A pretty stone house in the Karmen area of Dubrovnik that's perfect for a romantic getaway. It's a traditional city neighbourhood, where neighbours greet each other in the street, children play football in cobbled lanes and old women chat in doorways of stone houses. Owned by the energetic Karmen Sentić, this house is named after the area rather than the owner. The building has a history of survival, having seen off the 1667 earthquake and escaped damage during the 1991 siege. It once belonged to Karmen's aunt and her mother met her future husband on the street outside; now it's a charming house with a bedroom on each of the upper two floors (expect steep stairs), and a sitting-room with satellite TV and galley kitchen down. Once you have settled, Karmen will leave you to your own devices, but she's easy to reach if needed. You can judge a guest house by its repeat visits and Karmen's has plenty of these. You walk through pedestrianised city to reach it – Karmen or a family member will meet you and arrange a porter if necessary. And if you tire of cooking, dinner is available on request.

Self-catering

rooms	House for 4.
price	€80.
meals	Self-catering. Breakfast & dinner on request. Restaurants 200m.
closed	Never.
directions	Up steps to the Karmen area of Dubrovnik, bear left and into the winding alley towards the docks. House on left.

Karmen Sentić

tel	+385 (0)20 322 191
mobile	+385 (0)98 335 615
fax	+385 (0)20 322 192
email	karmen.sentic@kompas-travel.com
web	www.dubrovnik-online.com/house_karmen/

Map 8 Entry 125

Villa Adriatica

Frana Supila 4, Dubrovnik, 20000 Dubrovnik-Neretva

Stuffed with antiques, a grand piano, clocks, mirrors, paintings and an intriguing collection of gramophones, this villa is an unusually charming place to stay. Built next to Dubrovnik's Ploče Gate in the early 19th century, it remains remarkably unspoiled. In the authentically old-fashioned kitchen are fresh white walls and an old terracotta floor; in the sitting room, polished parquet. Adventurous cooks can test their skills on the traditional *peka* oven (food is protected by a domed metal plate, then covered with hot coals)… but there is an Aga-style burner *and* modern hob for the cheese-on-toast brigade. Bedrooms are fresh, white and tidy, with simple shower rooms; those at the back open onto a vast terrace, with stunning views across the harbour towards Lokrum Island and the sturdy bulwarks of Fort Sv Ivan. The apartment for two comes with its own kitchen and dining room, though is front facing and noisier. Large parties may rent the house as one. The owners, who live in a private wing, tend the garden, and are happy for you to pick lemons from the trees. Wonderful.

rooms	3 + 1: 3 doubles, sharing kitchen. 1 apartment for 2. Extra beds available.
price	€70–€100.
meals	Self-catering. Restaurants 200m.
closed	Never.
directions	Next to Ploče Gate, the southern entrance to the old city, in same building as Perla Adriatica travel agency.

Self-catering

	Teo Tomšić
tel	+385 (0)20 411 962
mobile	+385 (0)98 377 954
fax	+385 (0)20 422 766
email	miroslav.tomsic@du.htnet.hr
web	www.dubrovnik-online.com/villa_adriatica

Map 8 Entry 126

Sesame Inn

Don Frane Bulića 5, Dubrovnik, 20000 Dubrovnik-Neretva

The 200-year-old townhouse, a stroll from headland and sea, has been home
to the Ercegovićs since the early 1800s when the current owner's great-
grandparents moved in. It has an interesting history: plots were drawn up here
against the French occupation in 1808; later Grandfather, on the other side of the
family, won exclusive rights to sell alcohol. Now the family run a hugely popular
restaurant next door. Mihovil Ercegović makes a big effort to ensure diners are
well fed; Dalmatian and Mediterranean dishes dominate the menu, the wines
are local, and jazz evenings add a buzz to summertime dinners. Mihovil has other
strings to his bow: he owns an art gallery and is a photographer. The taverna's
exterior is handsomely dressed in local stone and hanging vines; the interiors
are well-proportioned and crisply modern, with excellent white shower rooms.
Casement windows look onto orange trees in the garden and a small, sunny
terrace, and a couple of bouncy golden retrievers help make you feel at home.
20% supplement for stays under three nights.

rooms	4: 3 doubles, 1 single.
price	€43.10–€57. Single €22.25–€30.56.
meals	Breakfast €4. Lunch & dinner €19.
closed	Never.
directions	150m up Dante Alighieri Street from Pile Gate.

Restaurant with rooms

	Mihovil-Miško Ercegović
tel	+385 (0)20 412 910
mobile	+385 (0)91 500 8647
email	misko.ercegovic@du.t-com.hr
web	www.sesame.hr

Map 8 Entry 127

Villa Ragusa
Žudioska 15, Dubrovnik, 20000 Dubrovnik-Neretva

The old stones hint at a fascinating history: Byzantine conquerors, Venetian seafarers, Jewish merchants. The family bought the house 200 years ago, but the foundations were laid in the 15th century. This was once the centre of the busy Jewish quarter and is in a great position: down a steep alley off Placa Stradun, a stroll from the grand municipal buildings on the harbour wall but away from the day trippers' tract. Behind these robust walls are angular rooms with exposed stonework, angel carvings on the lintels and hardwood floors polished to a sheen by centuries of use. There are exposed beams, regal canopied curtains and big windows – beyond which a sea of roofs glides down to the water, sprinkled with the domes of churches. The best views are from the top floor. Pero Carević is something of a wag and a keen conversationalist – but if you haven't the energy for a debate over breakfast, retreat to the local bar instead; there's an arrangement for alternative breakfasts there. *Supplement charged for stays of under three nights. Airport transfers for stays of one week.*

rooms	5: 3 doubles, 2 singles.
price	€50–€80. Singles €20–€40. Whole house €150–€300 per night.
meals	Breakfast €8. Restaurants 100m.
closed	Never.
directions	From Pile Gate, 300m east on Placa Stradun, left onto Žudioska. Villa signed on left.

	Pero Carević	B&B
tel	+385 (0)20 453 834	
mobile	+385 (0)98 765 634	
email	villa.ragusa@hi.htnet.hr	
web	villaragusa.netfirms.com	

Map 8 Entry 128

Vesna's Cottage
Lapadska 6, Lapad, Dubrovnik, 20000 Dubrovnik-Neretva

Surrounded by the sprawling suburbs of Lapad but screened by a lush walled garden, Vesna's Cottage is a little piece of countryside in the city. With ceiling timbers painted blue and green to mirror the garden, this striking structure grew out of the imagination of Vesna Mitrović, the effusive administrator of Club Otek, Dubrovnik's alternative arts centre. By day, she works as a graphic designer, sharing her artistic leanings with her photographer husband. By night, she pours her energy into festivals, art shows and cultural events. The creative streak is reflected in her house – unlike anything else we have seen in Croatia! Earthy materials and carefully chosen antiques mix beautifully with bold but natural colours. You get a bedroom, bathroom, kitchen and a living room with open fire. The family live next door and you share the half-tamed garden: brimming with fruits and flowers, it is a delight. The family is passionate about green issues and organic produce, making this a particularly lovely place for alternative and creative people to stay. *20% supplement for stays of under three nights.*

rooms	Cottage for 2.
price	€100–€140.
meals	Self-catering. Restaurants 200m.
closed	Never.
directions	From Gruž harbour, 200m northwest dir. Lapad penninsula. House on left, just before Villa Elisa Faculty of Economics.

Self-catering

	Vesna Mitrović
tel	+385 (0)20 356 078
mobile	+385 (0)91 738 8773
email	vesnascottage1@email.t-com.hr
web	free-du.t-com.hr/vesnascottage/

Map 8 Entry 129

Villa Miomir

Stonska 8, Lapad, Dubrovnik, 20000 Dubrovnik-Neretva

Good humour and generosity are the hallmarks here. Ivona Vlašić-Petrak is effusive and engaging, a gifted linguist who loves people and their stories. Her mother once owned the apartment upstairs; now Ivona has bought the whole house and added a cottage in the grounds. The villa dates back to the late 1920s, when imposing porches, shutters and wrought-iron balconies were in vogue, and sits in an enormous garden above street level, virtually hidden behind a vine-cloaked wall. It's peaceful here yet a short trot from the pedestrianised centre of Lapad, and near a popular shingle beach. The apartments have lofty ceilings and gleaming wooden floors and are refreshingly cool in summer. Imaginatively decorated bedrooms fuse modern trims with antiques and imported Indian pieces; the mood is vaguely colonial – exotic, not overpowering – and behind every ornament there's a story to tell (Ivona will need little prompting!). The apartments are in the main house, one with a balcony over the porch, one tucked under the roof; the cottage sits independently in the grounds.

rooms	2 apartments: 1 for 2, 1 for 3. Cottage for 4.
price	€50–€120.
meals	Self-catering. Restaurants 100m.
closed	Upstairs apartment closed December-March.
directions	From Pile Gate in Dubrovnik, 3km to Lapad; follow Ive Vojnovića to Kralja Tomislava. Bear left at fork: road becomes Kardinala Alojzija Stepinca. Straight on, cross Stonska; on left.

	Ivona Vlašić-Petrak
tel	+385 (0)20 438 582
email	ivonav@hotmail.com

Self-catering

Map 8 Entry 130

Apartment Bok

Kardinala Stepinca 44, Lapad, Dubrovnik, 20000 Dubrovnik-Neretva

A splendid private garden, spread over two levels and shielded from neighbours by hedges and trees, makes this one of the nicest private apartments near Dubrovnik. A covered terrace creates shade for lazy picnic lunches; on a higher level, trees provide pools of dappled light for outdoors snoozers. The apartment occupies the upper floor of the family home of Srećko Kržić and sits peacefully on a residential street on the Lapad peninsula. A lover of Italian culture and cuisine, Srećko took the apartment on as a creative project and has invested it with his unique sense of design. The walls of the main twin room are covered in fabulously kitsch pink roses, while picture windows frame the rooftops of Lapad and the sea beyond. Srećko works as a college professor, but his spare time is devoted to keeping the gardens and terraces lush; even the guest garden is a beautifully tailored space. It is great for families – three bedrooms, a well-equipped kitchen, a good bathroom – and you are close to the pedestrianised centre of Lapad and the popular municipal beach. *Minimum stay seven nights.*

Self-catering

rooms	Apartment for 5.
price	€700 per week.
meals	Self-catering. Restaurant 200m.
closed	Never
directions	From Pile Gate in Dubrovnik, 5km to Lapad; follow Ive Vojnovića to Kralja Tomislava. Bear left at fork: road then becomes Kardinala Alojzije Stepinca. Straight on, cross Stonska; on right.

	Srećko Kržić
tel	+385 (0)20 435 047
mobile	+385 (0)91 435 0477
email	srecko.krzic1@du.htnet.hr

Map 8 Entry 131

Villa Wolff

N. i M. Pučića 1, Lapad, Dubrovnik, 20000 Dubrovnik-Neretva

A pocket of chic in the midst of suburban bustle. Reached via steps at the tip of the Lapad peninsula, the former monastery dips its toes into the bay. According to legend, its position made this a haven for pirates, before the Ragusa Republic secured its hold over the Dalmatian coast. Today it is a corner of peace, privacy and exclusivity away from bustling Dubrovnik. The lovely flower- and lounger-strewn terrace is the setting for special occasion breakfasts of champagne, caviar and smoked salmon: master of the house Gonzales prides himself on proffering something rather special. At night, dine here, or indulge in a spot of gastro-hopping at pre-booked tables; there are plenty of good seafood restaurants in Dubrovnik. The mood is cosmopolitan; Gonzales himself is half Austrian, half Croatian, and his rooms have names plucked from Greek myths and legends. Bathrooms are snowy white; bedrooms, not huge, are fresh, light and new, some with earth and sky tones, some with balconies. The sea and palm views are a joy. *25% supplement for stays of under three nights.*

rooms	6: 3 doubles, 3 suites for 2-4.
price	€180–€200. Singles €180–€200. Suites €200–€240. Half-board extra €27 p.p.
meals	Lunch & dinner €25.
closed	November-March.
directions	From Dubrovnik, 5km to Lapad. Follow Ive Vojnovica to Kralja Tomislava, then left on (pedestrianised) Setaliste Kralja Zvonimira. Hotel signed on right, by bay.

	Gonzales Wolff
tel	+385 (0)20 438 710
fax	+385 (0)20 356 432
email	info@villa-wolff.hr
web	www.villa-wolff.hr

Hotel

Map 8 Entry 132

Apartment Magnolia

Od Greba Žudioskih 9, Dubrovnik, 20000 Dubrovnik-Neretva

With incredible views from the terraces over Dubrovnik's Old Town and the island of Lokrum, Dubravko's house stands in the shadow of Srd Mountain, a two-minute walk from the city walls. If you want heaps of space, a relaxed environment and stories to tell on your return home, it's ideal; less perfect if modish interiors are your thing! Built in the 1970s, there has been minimal renovation since. Many of the original features remain – beautiful tiles in the bathrooms and kitchens and parquet flooring throughout – and there are lots of plants and some wonderful pieces of furniture. The owner is not one to throw things out because they're no longer in vogue. A champion chess player in his youth, he traces his family back to the earthquake of 1667; his uncles and cousins live in neighbouring houses. English is not his forte, but his kindness helps fill the gaps and there's an English speaker to hand. The apartment takes up the whole of the top floor and you have the use of the tree-filled garden; access is through Dubravko's apartment below. *Minimum stay five to seven nights.*

rooms	Apartment for 7 (1 double, 1 twin, 1 triple).
price	€100–€150 per night.
meals	Restaurants 50m.
closed	Never.
directions	From Ploče Gate, cross road & head up hill. House almost at top, on left.

Self-catering

	Dubravko Zlošilo
tel	+385 (0)20 891 154
mobile	+385 (0)91 555 4003
email	magnolia9@net.hr
web	www.dubrovnik-online.com/apartment_magnolia

Map 8 Entry 133

Benussi Rooms & Apartments

Miha Klaića 10, Dubrovnik, 20000 Dubrovnik-Neretva

Rubbing shoulders with a 16th-century church in a stone alleyway behind the Hilton Hotel, the Benussi home is a beautifully preserved piece of old Dubrovnik. The stepped stone house has been in the family for generations; Jadranka and Milan live on one floor while the rest of the building is given over to the guest rooms and two tidy apartments. A cascade of terraces on one side allows views over a sea of terracotta tiles to the ocean beyond; one terrace is for guests, others are shared with the family. Enjoy the cool of the early evening as you swap stories with your sociable hosts. They have provided apartments and rooms they would be happy to live in themselves, as expressed in comforting colours and interesting details – a touch of exposed stone, a patchwork bedspread, a tiny stairway leading to a terrace. Greenery erupts at every turn, shrubs and trees peek unexpectedly from old stones. A long flight of steps connects the house to Ante Starčevića Street and from here it's only a five-minute stroll to Pile Gate and old Dubrovnik. *Longer stays preferred.*

rooms	2 + 2: 2 twins. 2 apartments: 1 for 4, 1 for 3.
price	330 Kn–480 Kn. Apartments 520 Kn–740 Kn per night.
meals	Restaurants 200m.
closed	Never.
directions	From Pile Gate, 7-minute walk west on Brsalje, passing Hilton Hotel. Right onto M. Klajića, follow around, pass church. Green door on right, signed.

	Jadranka Benussi
tel	+385 (0)20 429 339
mobile	+385 (0)98 928 1300
email	mbenussi@inet.hr
web	www.dubrovnik-online.com/apartments_benussi

Guest house & Self-catering

Map 8 Entry 134

Orhan Restaurant & Rooms

Od Tabakarije 1, Dubrovnik, 20000 Dubrovnik-Neretva

Strolling down the cobbled lanes to the seafront is like taking a step through time. Pale stone houses huddle together like fishwives waiting for the return of the fleet. Tucked below the mighty stone walls that have protected Dubrovnik since Venetian times is a small terrace of harbour buildings and the Orhan — one of the best restaurants in Dubrovnik. People cross town for the seafood: sea bream and crustacea fresh from the Adriatic and oysters from Ston. The gastronomy in the restaurant is matched by the unselfconscious charm of the old rooms in the house behind. They have wooden floors, white walls, comfortable beds and vintage furniture, and the best have sea views. Or you may prefer the six new rooms in a neighbouring building which, though smarter, lack the folksy charm. Owner Dominik Kuzman and sea-faring manager Matteo are a hospitable pair, but never intrude on your space; and Dominik's son Ivan speaks good English. Hard to imagine a better position, in a beautiful cove minutes from the walled old quarter but so peaceful that the sea will lull you to sleep. *Longer stays preferred.*

rooms	11: 9 doubles, 2 twins.
price	400 Kn.
meals	Breakfast 50 Kn. Dinner 100 Kn-150 Kn.
closed	Never. Restaurant closed Nov-Feb.
directions	From Pile Gate, walk south to waterfront. Follow shoreline path westwards for 25m.

Restaurant with rooms

	Ivan Kuzman
tel	+385 (0)20 414 183
fax	+385 (0)20 414 183

Map 8 Entry 135

Apartment House Dori

Rabljanina 5, Dubrovnik, 20000 Dubrovnik-Neretva

The streets of old Dubrovnik swim with people: locals back from market laden with still-warm bread and bags of crustacea, holiday makers shopping for a special something to take home. So it's nice to step back into a peaceful calm space you can call your own. Jadranka Petrović has created a warm and friendly apartment in an old stone house that feels lived in and loved – a brave recovery given that a grenade struck the roof in the Yugoslav War. It's a pretty building, its old stones and timbers dating from the 15th century, and although you can rent the whole house, most guests rent three-quarters of it: two double bedrooms, a living room, a good-sized kitchen/dining room (shared with Jadranka), pictures, hand-made sculptures and books. At the front is a tiny terrace with a table and chairs where you can sit out and enjoy the morning sunshine. Jadranka, an interesting woman and a charming hostess, occupies the third bedroom (most of the time) and will chat with you over coffee in the morning. So it's less self-catering, more house-sitting for a friend.

rooms	1 apartment for 4–6. Kitchen shared with owner. Whole house available.
price	€100–€160.
meals	Self-catering. Restaurants 20m.
closed	Never.
directions	From Pile Gate, along Stradun almost to Orlando's Column; right past Rector's Palace, right again past Gundulić Square; 1st right, past Sv Katarina church; on left up steps.

Self-catering

	Jadranka Petrović
tel	+385 (0)20 323 674
mobile	+385 (0)98 512 950
email	apartment_dori@net.hr
web	www.dubrovnik-online.com/apartment_dori/

Map 8 Entry 136

Summer Residence Mišetić

Šetaliste Marka Marojice 27, Mlini, 20207 Dubrovnik-Neretva

Step back in time to a 16th-century garden bordering the sea and filled with exotic blooms. The roll of the waves creates a delicious backdrop as you wander barefoot in the shade of the palms and flowering shrubs. On the serene shores of Župa Dubrovačka Bay, the Mišetić family's summer bolthole is a classic gothic-Renaissance villa, with an arched window set into the sea-facing wall and a shaded terrace overlooking the water. It has a turbulent history: it was damaged by an earthquake in 1667 and hit by a bomb in the recent war. No trace of these events remains, thanks to careful renovation by Marina Mišetić and her daughter Katarina. Both women have a personal connection to the house and gardens; they live on the ground floor and pop in regularly to water the plants and say hello. It is possible to rent the whole villa – kitchen, living room, four bedrooms – but many people like to rent individual rooms. Bedrooms have simple interiors: whitewashed walls, pressed linen, wrought-iron bedsteads and large shuttered windows opening onto the sea. *Minimum stay seven nights July / August. Bikes available for hire.*

rooms	4 doubles. Whole villa available.
price	€70–€100. Singles €40–€80. Villa €350–€500.
meals	Self-catering option. Cook available. Restaurants 1km.
closed	Never.
directions	From Dubrovnik, 15km east to Mlini turn-off. Signed on small road to shoreline; house on left.

B&B & self-catering

	Marina & Katarina Mišetić
mobile	+385 (0)98 880 685
fax	+385 (0)20 332 544
email	misetic@misetic.net
web	www.misetic.net

Map 8 Entry 137

Camping Kate
Tupina 1, Mlini, 20207 Dubrovnik-Neretva

The relaxed town takes its name ('Mills') from the grain and olive mills that are scattered across the slopes behind the boulder-fringed beach. Several small resorts along the coast have become popular in recent years; Mlini stands out for its fine sandy beaches and the regular ferry from Dubrovnik, saving visitors a slow, frustrating drive on the busy coastal road. Set in the pines and cypress trees behind the beach, Camping Kate is an old-fashioned, family-run camping ground, small-scale and friendly, where the focus is on families and gentle holidays by the sea. Plots are laid out in attractively landscaped grounds around an old stone house; soon there'll be a *konoba* serving local food. Trees fill the terraced camping areas and provide plenty of shade. Run with gusto by an engaging family, the site is the best option for campers in the Dubrovnik area – and the only camp with an environmentally-friendly ethos. Water in the smart shower block is heated by solar panels and the family run one of the few recycling projects in the region. *Extra charge for car parking, water & electricity.*

rooms	40 tents for 2-3.
price	€3.90–€5.10 p.p.
	Tent €2.35–€2.75.
	Caravan €3.17–€3.80.
	Discounts for under-18s.
meals	Restaurant 100m.
closed	November–April.
directions	From Dubrovnik, 8km south on road towards airport. Signed.

Camp

	Đivo Tomšić
tel	+385 (0)20 487 006
email	info@campingkate.com
web	www.campingkate.com

Map 8 Entry 138

Hotel Villa Kvaternik
Kvaternikova 3, Cavtat, 20210 Dubrovnik-Neretva

Up one side of the bay and down a winding stone alley is the Villa Kvaternik – a solid stone structure that dates from the 16th century. It is heritage listed, so owners Ken and Stan Medanić, Australians whose parents are Croatian, have kept the façade as they found it. It is the very essence of Dalmatian architecture: small windows, terracotta tiles, a patchwork of cut white stones. Inside, spacious bedrooms have soothing, summery colours; walls swim in blues and greens, mirroring the more riotous mosaic tiling in the bathrooms, and coloured bedspreads are turned back to reveal crisp white sheets. Pick a room colour to suit your temperament! Furniture is kept to a minimum, revealing gleaming wooden floors. On the ground floor is a breakfast terrace and a neatly-trimmed private garden. If there's no room in the hotel, you can stay in the annexe: a Franciscan monastery on the waterfront. Explore the peaceful cobbled streets that surround you, or rent the hotel's luxury motorboat for trips to local islands and Dubrovnik. *Minimum stay three nights May-September.*

Hotel

rooms	6: 5 doubles, 1 family suite for 4.
price	From €83.
meals	Restaurants 200m.
closed	Never.
directions	From Dubrovnik, 15 min south along the coast. Hotel is right in the centre of old Cavtat centre. Hotel accessed via steep steps.

Ken & Stan Medanić

tel	+385 (0)20 479 800
fax	+385 (0)20 479 808
email	sales@hotelvillakvaternik.com
web	www.hotelvillakvaternik.com

Map 8 Entry 139

Villa Sole

Prijeko 26, Cavtat, 20210 Dubrovnik-Neretva

As the annexe to Cavtat's Villa Magnolia, (see entry 141), Villa Sole has much to live up to. In the hands of Ivona Rajčević – whose indomitable great aunt, Marija, lived here to the age of 94 – it shines. On the exterior, the house is earthy, bold and Mediterranean; inside, it is a symphony of whites, ivories and delicate feminine detail. The bedrooms – two doubles – are gorgeous grand spaces of gilded mirrors, pine floors and pearly bed throws and cushions. The combination of rusticity and modernity is finely judged. You have an all-white kitchen, a sitting room with leather seating and sofabed opening onto a pergola-shaded terrace, and three sumptuous showers. Upstairs, a sun deck with loungers faces the forested headland across the bay. Stone walls screen the villa and its jewel of a courtyard garden (imagine citrus, jasmine, huge cacti) from the stepped, cobbled lanes outside. Ivona, who greets you on arrival and then leaves you to enjoy the peace, works for a travel agency in Dubrovnik and is a mine of local information. Make the most of her knowledge.

rooms	House for 4–6.
price	€120–€250.
meals	Self-catering. Restaurants 200m.
closed	Never.
directions	From town centre, north along promenade to 1st alley on right, by church; at top of several steps, left; house on right.

	Ivona Rajčević
tel	+395 (0)20 478 335
mobile	+385 (0)98 427 128
fax	+385 (0)20 478 335
email	ivona.rajcevic@du.t-com.hr
web	www.villa-sole.com

Self-catering

Map 8 Entry 140

Villa Magnolia
Prijeko 28, Cavtat, 20210 Dubrovnik-Neretva

From the palm-lined quayside, it's a 10-minute walk to the stone walls of this swooningly lovely Renaissance villa. A few houses back from the water, it has ravishing views of the bay, while sea breezes cool rooms as afternoon slips into evening. Built in 1704, it has seen several restorations. The previous owner established the clean white living spaces; now the Rajčević family have enhanced the interior with superb designer pieces. The mood recalls the 1960s, and there are some interesting quirks, such as the private chapel at the foot of the front garden, now bequeathed to the neighbouring church. You have three immaculate double bedrooms – a loving blend of old and new – a bath and a shower, a kitchen and a cream sofa'd living room. Outside: a charming courtyard garden, flower-filled and sea-facing. Dotted around are ancient cacti, orange trees, tresses of bougainvillea, mounds of lavender and a shady magnolia. A gentle stroll through stone-lined streets brings you to seafront tavernas. Wholly delightful.

Self-catering

rooms	House for 6-7.
price	€120–€250.
meals	Self-catering. Restaurants 200m.
closed	Never.
directions	From town centre, north along promenade to 1st alley on right, by church; at top of several steps, left; house on right.

Ivona Rajčević

tel	+395 (0)20 478 335
mobile	+385 (0)98 427 128
fax	+385 (0)20 478 335
email	ivona.rajcevic@du.t-com.hr
web	www.villa-sole.com

Map 8 Entry 141

Castelletto

Put od Cavtata 9a, Cavtat, 20210 Dubrovnik-Neretva

Three years ago, Castelletto was empty and unloved; what a difference today! The house gleams, with its pure white walls, arch-fronted terrace, bower of a garden and ocean or mountain view from every balcony. It is also filled with pretty reclaimed pine that Roger and Lesley brought with them from their business in Yorkshire; escaping to the Mediterranean was a life-long dream. Swapping Pennine rain for Adriatic sun was the easy part; transforming a modern war-scarred villa into an attractive guest house required energy and determination. Quilted bedspreads add an ethnic touch; large windows and sweeping floors make rooms feel airy and fresh; English books and games make you feel at home. Downstairs is the tapas restaurant and bar, spilling out into an enclosed garden with a barbecue for pork and lamb roasts, a lovely pool and cascades of flowers. Castelletto, 300 metres from the shore, is near the village of Cavtat, pretty with its double harbour and pine-cloaked headland. Dubrovnik is a boat or bus ride away and a hire car will open up the entire Dalmatian coast.

rooms	13: 10 doubles, 3 family rooms for 4.
price	€75–€95. Singles €55–€95. Family rooms €105–€115.
meals	Tapas dishes from 15 Kn. Restaurants 10-minute walk.
closed	Never.
directions	From Dubrovnik, 15km to Cavtat on the airport road. Signed on main road outside Cavtat.

	Lesley Smith	Guest house
tel	+385 (0)20 479 547	
fax	+385 (0)20 479 548	
email	lesley@dubrovnikexperience.com	
web	www.dubrovnikexperience.com	

Map 8 Entry 142

Zagreb & the interior: East marries West

Industrial Zagreb is Croatia's capital, the largest city in the country. Founded as two medieval settlements on two hills, it has a tangibly Viennese air, its architecture leaning more towards Austria and Hungary than the 'Venetian' towns along the coast. Culturally, too, Zagreb has long been a meeting point between east and west, and remains the nation's cultural hub. Among the stately civic buildings and formal parks of Donji Grad (the Lower Town) are national museums, theatres and galleries, while the pedestrianised Gradec district sees street festivals and a vibrant café and music scene. And the forested slopes of Mount Medvednica are a walker's paradise in summer and a major ski resort in winter.

In the northern region of Zagorje, vine-braided hills are relieved by a scattering of Hapsburg spa towns and medieval castles. The chapels that perch on hilltops here are a throwback to a time when the citizens considered the arduous climb towards heaven a testament to their faith in God. The views are inspirational, the gastronomy the pride of central Croatia. Zagorje's vineyards produce crisp white wines and rosés, and the cuisine has a subtle Central European influence.

Samobor has long been a favoured spot for day-trippers from Zagreb, with its winding rivers, elegant bridges and thriving café life. In the surrounding forests are remote ranches and a way of life marked by the changing seasons.

One of the best-loved places in the interior, Varaždin, is a baroque town just inside the Croatian border. A wealthy city in medieval times, Varaždin became an independent monarchic state in the 12th century and later served as the capital of Croatia. In September, during the Varaždin Baroque Evenings Festival, the town jumps with music and colour. Another highlight is the town cemetery, famed for its maze of tightly trimmed topiary.

Slunj, in the south, is a conservation area with a raw natural beauty. Two rivers meet at an island-strewn confluence scattered with watermills: this is Rastoke, one of the prettiest sights in the region, where rapids rush and churn.

Off to the east is the district of Slavonia, solidly rural and Eastern European in character. At its centre is Osijek, famous for the baroque Tvrda district by the river. Accommodation is mainly on farms and ranches; the independent-minded inhabitants of Slovonia are inclined towards self-sufficiency.

Zagreb & the interior

Hotel Risnjak
Lujzinska 36, Delnice, 51300 Karlovac

Lynx, bear, deer and boar – the forest is their home, and this hotel is heaven for all those in love with the wilds. In the style of an Alpine chalet, with its overhanging roof and wooden balconies, this modest-sized hotel backs onto the fir-covered slopes of the Risnjak massif, a playground for hikers, climbers, riders and nature lovers. In winter, long icicles hang from the eaves and snow reaches to the door. The hotel has seen subtle changes over the years, from slight austerity in the communist days to the warm mountain lodge you find today, and manager Silvia Sobol has done her job well, to inject new life into the place. Furniture is modern wicker or wood, bedrooms have floating muslin and white bed linen; some of the more luxurious rooms flaunt traditional carved bedsteads. Game and other local delights are served in the arch-filled dining room downstairs; across the hallway is a wood-panelled bar and a coffee shop with an après-ski mood – bliss to sit back with a glass of grappa after an afternoon scrambling in the woods. Outdoor activities are the thing here, from canoe safaris to canyoning.

Hotel

rooms	21: 5 doubles, 6 singles, 6 triples, 4 quadruples.
price	€48–€143.
meals	Breakfast €4. Lunch & dinner €8.
closed	Never.
directions	Rijeka-Zagreb, exit Delnice; 2km; hotel in centre of town.

	Silvija Sobol
tel	+385 (0)51 508 160
fax	+385 (0)51 508 170
email	info@hotel-risnjak.hr
web	www.hotel-risnjak.hr

Map 2 Entry 143

KADO Vila Kapela
Jasenak 86e, Ogulin, 47314 Karlovac

Little traffic disturbs the carefree mood at this modern chalet on a woodland lane near Ogulin. The village of Jasenak rides the ridge between Ogulin and the coast, surrounded by woods rich with nuts, berries and wild mushrooms. It is a backwater but in the best sense of the word; time is measured not in hours but in seasons. The house stands on the outskirts of the village, backed by forests that rise up to the Bjelolasica Natural Park, where athletes train for the winter and summer Olympics. Constructed in the traditional mountain style, it has dark timbers on stone foundations and is encircled by a covered stone terrace. Inside, all is spacious and pine-clad. The apartments have simple wooden furnishings and small kitchenettes, and the occasional wall is decorated with a pair of old wooden skis or a collages of branches and seeds. The young couple who manage the house live on site and can help you organise outdoorsy excursions – even when the forest is buried in snow. At Vrelo you have all the equipment you need for an adventurous summer or winter break. *20% supp. for stays of two nights and under.*

rooms	2 apartments for 4.
price	€104.
meals	Self-catering. Restaurant 2km.
closed	Never.
directions	From Karlovac, 55km south to Ogulin; 23km to Jasenak. Detailed directions on booking.

Self-catering

	Krešimir Pavić
tel	+385 (0)1 375 0476
mobile	+385 (0)91 338 3381
fax	+385 (0)1 3750 491
email	info@adriatic-turizam.hr
web	www.bjelolasica.net

Map 2 Entry 144

Ranch Jelov Klanac

Jelov Klanac bb, Rakovica, 47245 Karlovac

Rather more Scandinavian than Croatian, the attractive new building is decked in pine. It could be a Finnish chalet transplanted to the outskirts of the Plitvice Lakes National Park. Your ever-active hostess Blanka Pavlić has decorated her two light and airy apartments with understated good taste and masses of blond wood, from kitchen units to dining chairs. Colour comes from brick-red upholstery, living rooms are heated by free-standing stoves and there's little to disturb the peace, just birdsong and whinnying horses. To step out with a morning cup of coffee and spot these beautiful creatures galloping on the slopes makes for a perfect start to the day. The apartments are side by side, each with a small front terrace and an under-the-eaves balcony at each end of the house. Explore the National Park to your heart's content, negotiate racing rivers, ride horses through the woods, forage for wild mushrooms and strawberries, hike along rocky ridges. Or sit calmly on the river bank with a fishing rod and a flask of cocoa. Marvellous. *Minimum stay two nights. Bikes available for hire.*

Self-catering

rooms	2 apartments: 1 for 4, 1 for 6.
price	Apartment for 4, €100.
	Apartment for 6, €100–€140.
meals	Self-catering.
	Restaurants within 5km.
closed	Never.
directions	From Zagreb, 100km south to Slunj; 25km to Rakovica. In village, turn right after 500m; 7km to Jelov Klanac.

	Blanka Pavlić
mobile	+385 (0)98 704 612
fax	+385 (0)47 784 242
email	iriscroatica@gs.t-com.hr
web	www.jelovklanac.com

Map 2 Entry 145

Ruhige Lage
Oštarski Stanovi 125, Rakovica, 47245 Karlovac

The name – Peaceful Place – says it all. The setting is paradise. Mellow hills all around – guarding astonishing caverns hollowed out by centuries of rain – and deer grazing on the slopes. You are in the Plitvice Lakes National Park, most famous for its interconnecting waterfalls and pools. Vlado and Zdenka Božičević founded their country guest house as part of the rebuilding process following the Yugoslav War, planting it on their smallholding just outside the village. The new house fits comfortably into its surroundings – simple white walls, arched windows, sloping tiled roofs covering two vast terraces. There are three self-catering apartments here and one guest room; all have private terraces overlooking the countryside. Vlado has many talents; he crafted the cherrywood and ash furniture in the rooms and was once a professional chef. Breakfasts are a feast of hams and salamis, cheese and eggs from neighbouring farms; bread is baked daily by Vlado's mother. The family are very welcoming, and children will be happy with football field, table tennis and playground.

rooms	1 + 3: 1 triple.
	2 apartments for 4, 1 for 6.
price	€32–€40. Apartments €32–€96.
meals	Restaurants 400m.
closed	Never.
directions	From Zagreb, south towards Slunj, then 18km to Oštarski Stanovi, between Slunj & Plitvice. Detailed directions on booking.

B&B & Self-catering

	Zdenka Božičević
tel	+385 (0)47 784 135
mobile	+385 (0)91 525 0220
email	zdenka.bozicevic@ka.t-com.hr

Map 2 Entry 146

Ranch Winnetou Barilović

Barilović, 47252 Karlovac

This ranch in the forested hills above Karlovac is for tough nuts only. Damaged during the Yugoslav War, and missing out on the wave of farmhouse renovations that followed in this part of Croatia, it has no running water and limited electricity. Warmth comes from the camp fire, dinner from the bush kitchen (fish fresh from the river are cooked over the embers), and water from the spring. Eggs, milk and meat are home produced; no point shopping in the village when you have no fridge to keep things cool! Sleeping arrangements are similarly rustic: you bed down on simple bedsteads in cabins – or, should that prove to be a mite too comfortable, on mattresses on the barn floor. Showers are outside and wcs in; one cabin has its own bath. Owner also of Eko-Selo (see entry 154), Željko Milovanović has exciting plans for Winnetou but is happy for now to give you a taste of life as it was lived a century ago. As for adventure, there's plenty of that – trail riding, forest trekking, river swimming, foraging for wild foods. If you're lucky, you'll meet the family while you're here. Huge fun.

Ranch

rooms	12 beds in barn & cabins, most sharing showers. Camping for max.10.
price	Prices on application.
meals	Meals available. Restaurant 2km.
closed	Never.
directions	From Karlovac, 12km south to Barilović. From centre, cross 1st bridge over Korana; left, 1 km, signed.

	Marijana Milovanović
tel	+385 (0)1 338 7472
web	www.eko-selo.hr

Map 2 Entry 147

Hotel Korana

Perivoj J. Vrbanića 8, 47000 Karlovac

Four rivers converge on Karlovac, built as a stronghold against the Ottoman invasion and besieged seven times but never conquered. An attitude of indomitability has persisted: after the Yugoslav War, Karlovac picked itself up and rebuilt its fortune on beer. The Karlovačko label is now known across Croatia. The hotel stands just outside town, tucked into a bend of the Korana river: if you leave the windows open at night, the waters should lull you to sleep. It's a striking building, its towers and balconies protruding at unusual angles, and sits in large grounds. Much of the structure was damaged in the war, but the old hotel has been revived with careful attention to period detail, from the old-fashioned coffee shop to the riverside terrace. It's a genteel place to stay – rooms are airy, colours sober, bed linen crisp, and black and white bathroom tiles gleam. Staff are as courteous as you might expect from such a pristine place. Breakfasts include fresh local fruits; lunches and dinners are served on the terrace in summer, watching river boats and birds and sipping Croatian wines. *Bikes available for hire.*

rooms	18: 15 doubles, 3 suites.
price	730 Kn-990 Kn. Singles 870 Kn. Suites 990 Kn-1,350 Kn.
meals	Lunch & dinner 60 Kn-250 Kn.
closed	Never.
directions	From Zagreb, 37km southwest to Karlovac. Detailed directions on booking.

	Ivan Srakovčić
tel	+385 (0)47 609 090
mobile	+385 (0)91 521 6379
fax	+385 (0)47 609 091
email	info@hotelkorana.hr
web	www.hotelkorana.hr

Hotel

Map 2 Entry 148

Hotel Dvorac Bežanec

Valentinovo 55, Pregrada, 49218 Krapina Zagorje

It was built in the 17th century as the country seat of the Keglević family: a *dvorac* (castle) in the early baroque style, in grand forested grounds in the village of Valentinovo. In winter the grounds are cloaked in snow, romance is in the air, horses and deer roam. In spite of its architectural status, the old place found itself abandoned and facing the fate of so many others: neglect and ruin. Until 1990, when Siniša Križanec, who grew up in the area, arrived on the scene – Dvorac Bežanec's shining knight in armour. He purchased the lease and restored the palace to its former glory. Now it is one of Croatia's most memorable starred hotels. The interior is one great flourish of candelabras, antique upholsteries and fabulous, original works of art. Stately bedrooms come with period-style pieces; fabrics are soft to the touch; tall windows survey the grounds or inner courtyard. Wine cellar, bar, restaurant, writing room, library – all are yours to enjoy. There's horse riding, archery and balloon rides in the grounds... and the requisite friendly ghost.

Hotel

rooms	24: 20 doubles, 4 suites for 3-4.
price	597 Kn-697 Kn.
	Suite 697 Kn-897 Kn.
meals	Lunch & dinner 99 Kn-150 Kn.
	À la carte from 150 Kn.
closed	Never.
directions	From Zagreb, 47km; then Zabok-Krapinske road to Pregrada. Detailed directions on booking.

	Gordana Križanec
tel	+385 (0)49 376 800
fax	+385 (0)49 376 810
email	dvorac-bezanec@kr.htnet.hr
web	www.bezanec.hr

Map 2 Entry 149

Hotel Dvorak Gjalski

Gredice zabočke 7, Zabok, 49210 Krapina Zagorje

The country setting suits this cream-coloured manor perfectly. An impressive relic from the final days of feudalism, it was once the seat of the powerful Babić family, and the ancestral home of Ksaver Šandor Gjalski, who wrote so revealingly about the decline of aristocratic life. Almost mirroring his stories, the mansion was sold and ended up as a nightclub – until the current owners took it on and worked their magic. Every inch the country-house hotel, Dvorak Gjalski is dark and bohemian on the lower levels, bright and baroque on the upper. Grand mirrors reflect smart touches: striped drapes, leather chesterfields, reproductions of old icons. The atmosphere is both hotel-modern and classic. And there's masses of space, in bedrooms, bathrooms and picture-lined corridors. You have two restaurants here, one moody and gothic, one light, bright and filled with smart wrought-iron chairs, plus a covered *konoba* with wood-fired ovens in the grounds. Staff are good-humoured and professional. Forests, horse ranches and historic country towns are within easy reach, as is Zagreb.

rooms	21: 15 doubles, 2 triples, 2 suites.
price	495 Kn. Singles 363 Kn. Suites 605 Kn.
meals	Lunch & dinner 60 Kn-100 Kn.
closed	Never.
directions	Zagreb-Maribor exit Zabok; hotel signed.

	Spomenko Vida	
tel	+385 (0)49 201 100	
mobile	+385 (0)98 953 4947	
fax	+385 (0)49 201 135	
email	gjalski@post.t-com.hr	
web	www.dvorac-gjalski.hr	

Hotel

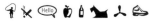

Map 2 Entry 150

Lojzekova hiža

Gusakovec 116, Gornja Stubica, 49245 Krapina Zagorje

Pilgrims have been coming to Marija Bistrica since the 13th century to see the statue of the Virgin Mary, long credited with miraculous powers. Christians still come in huge numbers, joined by a new kind of pilgrim – holiday makers in search of deep country. Lojzek's House has a laid-back farmhouse charm. And yet it was built just a decade ago, using craftsmen versed in the art of traditional methods. Vintage pieces of farm machinery and quirky wooden furniture add to the illusion of age. The welcome is genuine though! Pavica and Darko combine a boundless energy with a naturally relaxed style, so both house and grounds are a playground for their children as well as yours – along with the animals. In the middle of all this, Pavica finds time to prepare fine country meals in her wood-lined *konoba*, using produce from the farm and, in season, gathered mushrooms. Dishes are spread on red gingham tablecloths in a Hansel and Gretel dining room. Bedrooms are very simply furnished in keeping with the mood; shuttered windows open to leafy gardens and window boxes spill with flowers.

Guest house

rooms	9: 3 doubles, 6 family rooms for 4.
price	240 Kn. Family room 480 Kn. Discount for children; under sixes free.
meals	Half-board 180 Kn p.p. Full-board 210 Kn p.p.
closed	Never.
directions	Zagreb to Gornje Stubice, 45km; road to Marija Bistrica, 4km; turn at Gusakovec for Lojzekova hiža.

Darko Grden

tel	+385 (0)49 469 325
mobile	+385 (0)98 250 592
fax	+385 (0)49 469 325
email	lojzekova.hiza@kr.t-com.hr
web	www.lojzekovahiza.com

Map 2 Entry 151

Pansion Puntar

Trg Sv Juraja 12, Gornja Stubica, 49245 Krapina Zagorje

East of Zabok, small roads wind through the countryside to castles and farmsteads that have barely changed since medieval times. In the quaint village of Gornja Stubica, within walking distance of Orsić Castle, Puntar is a typical down-to-earth, dependable inn that you find in country villages across Europe. Biserka Drempetić and family run the place with a friendly efficiency, keeping rooms cobweb-free and simmering good food on the stove. Bedrooms are simple affairs, with clean white walls, simple wooden furniture and cheery bedspreads, and the spacious studio has a cow skin rug which will fascinate small children. The family live nearby in a lovely old village house and guests are invited to explore their fruit gardens and vineyards, even to help out with picking the grapes. Less active types can sample the fruits of their labour in the restaurant, in the form of delicious wine and sweet brandy. Most of the food served here is home-grown or locally sourced, and organic. For something a little bit different, ask about sleeping in the hayloft in summer – a truly rustic experience.

rooms	6: 5 doubles, 1 studio.
price	240 Kn. Singles 150 Kn. Half-board extra 35 Kn p.p. Full-board extra 75 Kn p.p.
meals	Lunch & dinner 25 Kn-100 Kn.
closed	Never.
directions	Zagreb-Krapina, exit Zagreb; 10km to Gornja Stubica. Detailed directions on booking.

Restaurant with Rooms

	Filip Drempetić
tel	+385 (0)49 289 286
mobile	+385 (0)91 587 93 86
fax	+385 (0)49 289 286
email	pansion@puntar.hr
web	www.puntar.hr

Map 2 Entry 152

Kurija Medven

Medvenova Draga 13, Kostanjevac, 10455 Zagreb Region

The Medven family have lived in Kostanjevac long enough to have streets named after them. Their imposing manor house stands in sprawling grounds on Medvenova Draga; there's a sense of history in the air. The estate was constructed in 1868 and most of the original features remain, including the wine press and brandy still and a number of solid barns, topped by old-fashioned haylofts. Around the corner is the family water mill, still grinding after 200 years; one outbuilding has been converted into two guest apartments, kitted out in traditional style, with handmade furniture, firm, sleep-inducing wooden beds and ethnological relics hung about the walls. Your host is a talkative, energetic man who speaks limited English but still manages to impart a sense of enthusiasm and unfeigned hospitality. Rooms (with kitchenettes) are rented out on a B&B basis but a local cook stops by to prepare meals that are totally authentic for the region – lots of fire-cooked meat and game and bread prepared with flour ground in the family mill. There's still a sense that the family like to do things their own way today.

rooms	2 apartments: 1 for 3, 1 for 4.
price	360 Kn–480 Kn.
meals	Lunch & dinner 30 Kn-100 Kn.
closed	Never.
directions	Zagreb-Karlovac, exit Jastrebarsko. Follow old Karlovac road dir. Krašić for 4km. Detailed directions on booking.

B&B

Milivoj Medven

tel	+385 (0)1 627 0347
mobile	+385(0)98 920 1876
fax	+385 (0)1 627 0665

Map 2 Entry 153

Eko-Selo Žumberak

Koretići 13, Bregana, 10432 Zagreb Region

At first glance, Eko (as in Eco) Selo looks like a pristine 19th-century village – in a clearing in a valley beside a rushing stream. Horses trot calmly along the dirt road and dogs doze in the shade of picket fences on the lanes leading to the pitch-roofed cabins; each structure was moved here, lock, stock and barrel, from elsewhere in the area. Eko Selo lies deep in the Žumberak Natural Park and was created by the owners, Željko and Marijana Milovanović, as a wilderness camp. The old village of Žumberak was destroyed by fire in 1793; now the camp is bringing people back to this wonderful forested area. Half eco-village, half horse ranch, it is a brilliant place to stay if you love hiking, mountain biking, climbing, caving and especially riding. You stay in large cabins lined with timber – the scent of pine hits you as you enter – and beds are cosy with woollen blankets to keep off night chill. The apartments and cabins, sparsely furnished but snug, one with a kitchenette, are arranged around a log cabin restaurant. Forest trails and waterfall tours start from the door. *Ask about cowboy weddings.*

rooms	4 apartments: 2 for 2, 2 for 3. 5 cabins for 6, some sharing showers.
price	200 Kn–400 Kn. Cabins from 400 Kn.
meals	Lunch & dinner 20 Kn–80 Kn.
closed	Never.
directions	From Zagreb, 20km dir. Ljubljana; exit near Samobor; 7km towards Bregana. Detailed directions on booking.

Ranch

	Marijana Milovanović
tel	+385 (0)1 338 7472
web	www.eko-selo.hr

Map 2 Entry 154

Trajbar Team

Bana J. Jelačića 199, Zaprešić, 10290 Zagreb Region

Equestrians and nature-lovers gather at the Trajbar Team equestrian club for the thrill of riding beautiful horses through the forests around Zagreb. The stables and lodge are wrapped up in greenery, a short drive from the capital but a world away in mood and atmosphere. First-timers can learn to ride from scratch, while a network of peaceful forest trails awaits more experienced riders. Many guests are families with children; others are wedding parties, seduced by the chance of a romantic open-air service and the opportunity to arrive in a horse-drawn carriage. Overnight visitors stay in a purpose-built ranch tucked up against a wall of forest. Stables are in one long wing beside the show-jumping and dressage ground, while the restaurant and rooms occupy a comfortable red-roofed ranch house. The equestrian theme continues inside, with paintings of horses and riders on the walls and white furniture that adds to the bright, light feeling. Rooms are often booked out together for equestrian competitions and weddings. The dreamy honeymoon suite has a bed screened by billowing drapes.

Ranch

rooms	6: 5 twins, 1 suite.
price	320 Kn–420 Kn.
meals	Breakfast 30 Kn.
	Lunch & dinner 100 Kn.
closed	Never.
directions	From Zagreb Podsused, 17km west towards Zaprešić. Property on main road, on left after a stretch of woodland.

	Maja Trajbar
tel	+385 (0)1 331 0838
mobile	+385 (0)98 280 706
fax	+385 (0)1 331 0837
email	info@kk-trajbar-team.hr
web	www.kk-trajbar-team.hr

Map 2 Entry 155

Ilički Plac Private Accommodation

Britanski Trg 1, Zagreb, 10000 Zagreb Region

Zagreb's spanking new municipal trams run regularly from Ban Jelačić Square to this old-fashioned apartment building overlooking the Ilički Plac market. A Zagreb institution, the market sells fruit and veg during the week, and antiques and bric-a-brac on Saturdays. Many of the black and white photos and bits and pieces that dot Munira Serdarević's apartment were picked up here; the apartment has a cheerfully erratic décor to match the bohemian spirit of its owner. Munira once owned a wedding flower-arranging business; today, an assiduous collector of brocante, she devotes her time to collecting and restoring. The house has two twin rooms and a new single bedroom at the back, decorated in an unflashy style that goes back to the bourgeois Thirties and Forties. The large windows that overlook the market admit plenty of light and surprisingly little noise. This is not luxury accommodation, but it has an interesting history and you are bang in the centre of lively Zagreb. *10% supplement for stays of under three nights.*

rooms	3: 2 twins, 1 single.
price	405 Kn. Single 270 Kn.
meals	Breakfast not available. Restaurants 200m.
closed	Never.
directions	Trams: 2, 4, 6 from Ban Jelačić Square. By car, north down Ilica Street; Britanski Trg on right.

Rooms

	Munira Serdarević
mobile	+385 (0)98 419 231
email	ilicki@email.t-com.hr
web	www.ilicki.com

Map 2 Entry 156

Organic Farm Zrno
Habijanovac 45, Nova Kapela, 10343 Zagreb Region

The organic farm run by Zlata Nanić, on the edge of the horseshoe-shaped village of Habijanovac, is a pioneer of Croatia's burgeoning eco-tourism movement. Here, in the countryside east of Zagreb, the first ever Croatian award for sustainable farming was won. The farm's crops include rye, pir, fruits, berries and vegetables, nurtured with love and plenty of home-produced compost. Clever, good-natured, and with a charming twinkle in her eye, Zlata started Zrno when planning a trip to India. She is quite the visionary. You experience a totally natural way of living here — meals come only from organic, home-grown and vegetarian produce, and there's a wide range of holistic courses to choose from, from macrobiotic cooking to foraging from nature. Carnivores are treated to home-reared meat; small guests may enjoy the goats trotting around the farm. (And there are cats and dogs to fuss over, too.) You get three rustic guest rooms in the farmhouse, and a simple dining room with a guest kitchen. Wonky beams and hand-woven rugs add to the country mood, storks nest just outside.

rooms	3: 1 twin, 2 triples sharing showers. Guest kitchen.
price	Full-board €30–€40 p.p.
meals	Full-board only.
closed	Never.
directions	Directions on booking.

Guest house

	Zlata Nanić	
tel	+385 (0)1 272 8137	
mobile	+385 (0)91 272 8173	
fax	+385 (0)1 272 8196	
email	zlata.nanic@zg.t-com.hr	
web	www.bio-zrno.hr	

Map 3 Entry 157

Ravlić Agroturizam

Mužilovčica 72, Kratečko, 44213 Sisak-Moslavina

A fairytale welcome at this agroturizam, which lies in a sleepy village of preserved wooden houses in the wetlands of the Lonjsko Polje Nature Reserve. The winding Sava river has spawned a series of oxbow lakes, stocked with fish and covered by sheets of water lilies. The farmhouse could be straight out of Hans Christian Andersen, a 200-year-old cottage drenched in ivy and surrounded by songbirds. Across from the house is a traditional *kuvama*, a charmingly ramshackle wooden barn for mealtimes. Zlata Ravlić remembers coming here as a child with her musician dad to share slices of Turopolje ham and fire-grilled carp with the labourers. Inside are two rustic bedrooms heated by cast-iron wood-fired stoves and decorated with family furniture, duvets stuffed with down from the farm geese, and embroidered sheets passed down through generations of Ravlićs. Then there's the kitchen, where delightful Zlata prepares a superb range of dishes from old family recipes – with hams and salamis on sale in the farm shop. Boating, riding, walking and fishing await. *Supplement for single night stays.*

rooms	2: 1 single, 1 triple.
price	Single 145 Kn. Triple 290 Kn.
meals	Breakfast 25 Kn. Dinner from 60 Kn.
closed	Never.
directions	From Sisak, southeast along River Sava towards Jasenovac, through Čigoč & Kratečko.

	Ravlić Family
tel	+385 (0)44 710 151
fax	+385 (0)44 710 151
email	jaksa.ravlic@sk.htnet.hr

Guest house

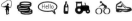

Map 3 Entry 158

Hotel Mozart

Kinkovo bb, Virovitica, 33404 Virovitica-Podravina

Perhaps it was the baroque church of Sv Roko in Virovitica that lured Jadranka from her native Vienna to this peaceful corner. Austro-Hungarian influence has always flowed freely between Austria and the Bilogora hills. Her upmarket hotel is set in quiet, wooded country by a small man-made lake: modern on the outside, unashamedly baroque within. Communal spaces shine with repro touches and the modern facilities are first-class; tan your tummy in the solarium, steam in the sauna, relax in the jacuzzi, and finish off with a well-earned glass of Croatian wine in the cellar, which is lined with polished tree trunks and burnished pine. Overlooking the lawns is a pink and white dining room, dotted with chandeliers, fringed by ruffled curtains. Bedrooms are less ornate and the calming Viennese colour scheme makes it a pleasure to linger. Black and white tiled bathrooms and veneered parquet add 1940s touches. Three rooms at the top create one smart suite – deep-pile carpeting and a corner bath in the main room. An invigorating small hotel, whose staff are on a mission to please. *Bikes available for hire.*

Hotel

rooms	27: 25 doubles, 1 single, 1 suite for 3.
price	600 Kn. Single 495 Kn. Suite 1,125 Kn.
meals	Lunch & dinner 30 Kn-120 Kn.
closed	Never.
directions	From Bjelovar to Virovitica on main road ("magistrala") to Podravska; through Špišic Bukovica; 3km.

Jadranka Đebro
tel +385 (0)33 801 000
fax +385 (0)33 801 016
email info@hotelmozart.hr
web www.hotelmozart.hr

Map 4 Entry 159

Hotel Vinarija

Vinogradska 102, Brodski Stupnik, 32253 Vukovar-Sirmium

A treat for connoisseurs of wine, the hotel sits on hallowed ground – as far as Croatian children are concerned. The winelands were the setting for the misadventures of a famous children's story character, Hlapić the Apprentice. These days, the Zdjelarević estate is more for the grown-ups; vineyard tours and other grape-related activities flourish. In a wide valley between rolling hills, this winery hotel is surrounded by a sea of coiled vines heavy with grapes. It was one of the first private vineyards in Croatia, established shortly before the Yugoslav War; previously, wine-making had been controlled by state-owned institutions. The estate quickly gained a reputation for superior rieslings and chardonnays. Behind the tidy modern frontage lie smallish rooms with a rustic feel – dark Slavonian-style furniture, iron wall lamps, parquet floors – with vineyard views from many windows. Creative Slavonian cooking is served in the restaurant, accompanied by the full range of Zdjelarević wines. In the grounds is a one-roomed chapel dedicated to Sv Klara, built after a storm destroyed an entire season's harvest.

rooms	15: 5 doubles, 7 singles, 3 triples.
price	580 Kn. Single 395 Kn. Triple 750 Kn-1,025 Kn.
meals	Lunch & dinner from 40 Kn.
closed	December.
directions	From Zagreb-Slavonski Brod highway, exit Lužani. After toll, right towards Slavinski Brod, then left towards Lovčić. Guest house 1km from turn-off.

Magdalena Azapović

tel	+385 (0)35 427 775
fax	+385 (0)35 427 040
email	vinarija-zdjelarevic@sb.htnet.hr
web	www.zdjelarevic.hr/hr/index.asp

Hotel

Map 4 Entry 160

Family Rural Economy Lacković

Vinogradska 5a, Bilje, 31327 Osijek-Baranja

The Lacković farm suffered its share of scars in the Yugoslav War, but you wouldn't know it now – all has been restored. The name of this country farmstay gives some idea of the pleasing, rural mood. Gardens are cheerful and lived-in, the family dog, cats, goats, geese and chickens gambol like lords of the manor and there's a huge vegetable patch from which the Lacković family produce organic food for the dining table. The big appeal here is the undisturbed tranquillity just ten minutes from Osijek. The house looks towards the marshlands of the Kopački Rit natural park; don't be alarmed to see the heads of monster pike caught in the surrounding lakes mounted as trophies on the walls. Guest rooms are just what you would expect from a small farm – simple, homely spaces with warm blankets and small, low beds. The welcome is warm and genuine and everyone sits down to eat together in the evening – generally to a hearty spread of Slavonian home cooking and produce from the farm. Predictably, and happily, freshly-laid eggs appear on the breakfast table every morning. *Bikes available for hire.*

rooms	4: 3 twins, 1 quadruple.
price	268 Kn. Quadruple 134 Kn p.p.
meals	Lunch & dinner 30 Kn–100 Kn.
closed	Never.
directions	Zagreb highway to Sl. Brod; continue to Velika Kopanica; main road left to Osijek, signed Bilje. Detailed directions on booking.

Guest house

	Srđan Lacković
tel	+385 (0)31 750 850
mobile	+385 (0)98 650 006
fax	+385 (0)31 751 329
email	andjelko.lackovic@os.htnet.hr

Map 5 Entry 161

Hotel Central

Trg A. Starčevića 6, Osijek, 31000 Osijek-Baranja

You don't get more central than this hotel overlooking the broad main square in the heart of Osijek. On the same block, the tall, gothic town cathedral punches skywards in a cascade of flying buttresses; down the road are the intriguing lanes of the Tvrda quarter, lined with grand bohemian architecture. All around, elegant townhouses with wrought-iron porch lanterns. Many of the hotel's original Art Nouveau details were lost or covered up during the austere years of socialist Yugoslavia, but the owners are slowly trying to recreate the baroque mood. You enter through a vast hallway, leading to a lobby and one of the last Viennese-style coffee houses in Osijek – all red velour upholstery and filigree picture rails. Bedrooms upstairs lack that old-world charm, but are still comfortable and well-equipped. All have heavy curtains, tidy wooden trim, fitted beds, and the odd throwback to socialist-era styling. Some of the top rooms look across to the cathedral; at the back is a small garden for concerts and cultural events. Charming, genuinely attentive staff ensure guests return.

rooms	39: 18 doubles, 21 singles.
price	514 Kn. Singles from 335 Kn. Half-board extra 50 Kn p.p.
meals	Half-board option at neighbouring restaurant.
closed	Never.
directions	From Osijek train station, north on Stjepana Radića, then left on Europska Avenija to Trg A. Starčevića (the main square).

Hotel

	Sandra Jakelić
tel	+ 385 (0)31 283 896
fax	+385 (0)31 283 891
email	hotel-central@os.htnet.hr
web	www.hotel-central-os.hr

Map 5 Entry 162

National Holidays & Festivals

Croatia follows the Roman Catholic calender of national holidays. Thanks to an additional number of independence days and regional festivals, Croatians enjoy almost three weeks of authorised rest per year.

New Year's Day:
1 January
Epiphany:
6 January
Carnival:
February – a lively, pre-Lent celebration with music, dancing, performance and fancy dress
Easter:
March/April
Labour Day:
1 May
Corpus Christi:
10 June
Day of Anti-Fascist Resistance:
22 June (marks the partisans' 1941 push)
Statehood Day:
25 June
Victory Day and National Thanksgiving Day:
5 August
Feast of the Assumption:
15 August
Independence Day:
8 October
All Saints' Day:
1 November
Christmas:
25/26 December

Photo Hotel Vinarija, entry 160

Language and glossary

Croatian is a Slavic language, belonging to the South Slavic languages group, and can be traced back to the 9th century. The standard language is based on the štokavski dialect; in Dalmatia, Istria and on the islands the čakavski dialect is used; and in Zagreb and Zagorje you will hear the kajkavski dialect, named each after the question 'what?' (što, ča and kaj in each case). Italian is also widely spoken in Istria. Some of your hosts will speak perfect English (and German, French and Italian, for that matter) while others will speak none at all. If this is the case, they will usually be able to find someone who can speak English. In this book we have striven to incorporate diacritics where they apply; we apologise for those we may have missed out.

Although it's rare to find a Croatian who does not speak some kind of second language, any efforts you make in the native tongue will be hugely appreciated.

Croatian words are pronounced exactly how they are spelt. This may not be such great advice to those who are having trouble reading Croatian but it is just a reminder that all letters and syllables in words are pronounced and there are no silent letters (unlike in English!). As a general rule of thumb, Croatian vowels are short. There is no q, w, x or y in the Croatian alphabet.

Pronunciation

a like a in sofa	i like ee in feet
c like ts in lets	j like y in yacht
č (hard) like ch in church	lj like l in lure
ć (soft) like ch in cheese	nj like Spanish ñ
dž similar to J in June	o like o in dog
đ like j in jam	u like oo in boot
e like e in met	r trilled
g like g in game	š like sh in sheep
h like h in ham	ž like s in measure

Useful words and expressions

Hello	Dobar dan	Do you speak English?	Govorite li engleski?
Goodbye	Doviđenja	I don't understand	Ne razumijem
How are you?	Kako ste?	How much?	Koliko košta?
My name is	Zovem se	Do you have...?	Imate li?
I am from	Ja sam iz	I'm vegetarian	Ja sam vegetarijanac
What is the time?	Koliko je sati?		

Language and glossary

Bon appetit!	Dobar tek!	Ulje	oil
Thank you	Hvala	Maslinovo ulje	olive oil
Please	Molim	Ocat	vinegar
Excuse me/ sorry	Oprostite	Juha	soup
Yes	Da	Sir	cheese
No	Ne	Rižot	risotto
When?	Kada?	Tartufe	wild truffles
Where is?	Gdje je?		
How go I get to?	Kamo idem?	Drinks	
How far is it to?	Koliko je daleko?	Voda	water
One	Jedan	Kava	coffee
Two	Dva	Čaj	tea
Three	Tri	Mlijeko	milk
Four	Četri	Vino	wine
Five	Pet	Pivo	beer

Menu decoder

Basics		Fish	
Restoran	restaurant	Riba	fish
Doručak	breakfast	Brodet	fish stew
Ručak	lunch	Lignje	squid
Večera	dinner	Losos	salmon
Šećer	sugar	List	sole
Pecivo	bread roll	Kovač	John Dory
Kruh	bread	Brancin	sea bass
Kolač	cake	šaran	carp
Palačinke	sweet pancakes	Pastrva	trout
	filled with jam	Jastog	lobster
	or chocolate	Lignje	squid
Maslac	butter	Bakalar	pâté/spread
Pekmez	jam		made from dried
Med	honey		cod
Jaje	eggs		
Tjestenina	pasta	Meat	
Riža	rice	Meso	meat
Sol	salt	Govedina	beef
Papa	pepper	Janjetina	lamb

Kunić	rabbit
Piletina	chicken
Svinjetina	pork
Čevapčići	meatballs
Kulen	spicy salami
Pršut	home-cured ham or proscuitto

Vegetables

Krumpir	potato
Grah	beans
Mahune	French beans
Grašak	peas
Kupus	cabbage
šampinjoni	mushroom
Luk	onion
Češnjak	garlic
Rajčica/paradajz	tomato
Krastavac	cucumber
(Zelena) salata	(green) salad

Useful phrases

Mam rezervaciju za... I have a room reserved in the name of...

Imate li slobodnih soba?
Do you have any rooms free?

Trebao(/la) bih I would like a...
...jednokrevetnu sobu
...single room
...dvokrevetnu sobu
...double room

Uzet ću sobu na jednu noć.
I'll take the room for one night.

Koliko košta soba za jednu noć?
How much is the room per night?

Koliko košta soba po osobi?
How much is the room per person?

Da li je doručak uključen?
Is breakfast included?

U koliko sati je doručak
What time is breakfast?

Kako je daleko plaža?
How far is the beach?

Pet minuta hoda.
It is 5 minutes walk.

Da li je plaža pješčana ili šljunkovita?
Is the beach sandy or rocky?

Kako je daleko centar grada?
How far away is the town centre?

Zelio bih platiti račun.
I would like to pay my bill.

Mogu li platiti sa kreditnom karticom?
Can I pay by credit card?

Primate li Visa ili Mastercard karticu?
Do you accept Visa or Mastercard?

Glossary of places

Konoba	Tavern
Torci	Olive Press
Kažun	Shepherd's shelter
Tornjica	Smoke house
Peka	Traditional oven
Dvorac	Castle or mansion

With thanks to
www.visit-croatia.co.uk

History and culture

As a strategic point of access between Eastern and Western Europe, Croatia has attracted the attention of many nations. Istria's caves were occupied from the Palaeolithic era; then, during the Bronze Age (3,500 BC-1,200 BC), the population soared, as testified by the remnants of 400 hill forts. The Vučedol culture stretched from Eastern Slavonia to the Czech Republic and across to Germany, before spreading down to the islands of the Adriatic.

Of the early civilisations it is the Illyrians who are the best documented. An Indo-European people who settled in Dalmatia around 1000 BC, they were eventually conquered by the Romans. These, in turn, came to rule the entire Balkan area – Serbia, Croatia, Bosnia, Slovenia, Montenegro, Bulgaria, Albania – and many signs of their occupation remain. Among the most notable are the amphitheatre in Pula and Emperor Diocletian's magnificent summer palace in Split.

The fall of the Roman Empire in the 5th century led to the arrival of a host of marauders. Huns, Goths, Bulgars, Avars and Vlachs were eventually superseded by the Croat tribe, who shared the marshy flatlands north of the Carpathian mountains with their fellow Slavs before migrating south into Dalmatia and Pannonia. At the same time, the Serbs and the Slovenes conquered those areas to which they would later lend their names.

Croatia prospered between 900 and 1100, as Dalmatia united with Slavonia and Bosnia to form one flourishing empire. It was not to last: separate initiatives from Byzantium and Venice claimed much of the coastline while Hungary captured the interior. In 1102 the Hungarian king persuaded the 12 most influential Croatian clans to sign a covenant that preserved their customs and traditions while agreeing to his rule, a treaty that would endure for 700 years.

Croatia's government remained fragile throughout this period, its leadership drawn from whichever country was the most powerful at the time. Croatian buildings are a testament to its occupied past: Austria, Hungary, the Ottoman Empire, Venice and the Hapsburgs can all be traced through the country's architecture.

Photo Chris Lucas

Attempts to overthrow the occupiers, whether made by aristocrats or serfs, were quickly quashed, though a few enclaves managed to stave off marauders and claim some semblance of independence. The Uskok pirates ruled the central coast for much of the 16th century, with local support, while Dubrovnik (or Ragusa as it was then known), paid off would-be claimants. Napoleon drove Croatia's occupiers away during his reign, only for Hapsburg rule to be reinstated after his fall, in 1815.

During the 19th century Croatian or 'Illyrian' culture experienced something of a renaissance, with traditional language and customs encouraged and revived by its rulers. The Viceroy of Croatia's ill-fated attempt to invade Hungary during the middle of the century backfired, allowing both countries to fall into Austria's hands. The Balkans came under intensive fire during World War I. At the end of the war, Croatia saw the state of the defeated Austro-Hungarian Empire, and joined with Serbia and Slovenia to form one nation under monarchic rule. This would become Yugoslavia. But until World War II the area was a political mess, with rival factions at odds as to how to divide the territory, until it was invaded by Germany in 1941.

Yugoslavia lost a tenth of its citizens – close to an estimated million Serbs, Croats, Muslims and Jews – during World War II, caught between the fascist Ustaše party, the Nazi occupiers, the partisans and the popular Tito-led Communist party. Thus, when the war ended in 1945, the people gladly elected Tito as their leader. Unifying the nations while simultaneously allowing each of the six republics autonomy over their state affairs, these solidifying powers disintegrated after his death in 1980. Yugoslavia's infrastructure proved weak without a centralising ruler and the country endured the bloody conflict of the Yugoslav War between 1991 and 1995. A decade on, Croatia has emerged stronger, savvier and with a more clearly defined national identity than ever. The country has shaken off the restraints of communism to welcome visitors from across the world, its arts and its agriculture prosper and, some say, Croatia may in the near future be claiming its seat in the EU.

Photo Renco Kosinoœiå Croatian Tourist Board

Croatia's rich pickings

Croatia's fertile earth and waters yield some of the most sumptuous produce in Europe. Farm shops, delicatessens and restaurants, where food is locally sourced and often organic, promise an array of flavours and textures unique to the country.

Expect fine olive oils, the drupes (fruits) hand-washed by farmers in the sea; wines from some of viticulture's earliest grapes; truffles from the iron-rich earth; honey from boutique apiaries; wild asparagus; Bora wind-cured ham; and seafood so fresh it revives the palate. These are some of the delicacies that are beginning to catch the attention of the world's culinary stage. Even Italians are popping over to see their Croatian neighbours in search of particular foods.

Photo Renzo Kosinoîlč, Croatian Tourist Board

Croatian wine and olive oil production dates back to pre-Christian times. The Roman emperors deemed that only olive oil from the 'golden triangle' between Vodnjan, Barbariga and Faožana was fine enough to grace the table; today, the owners of Jelsa's Pansion Murvica (entry 101) win awards for their olive oil and Novigrad's Torci 18 (entry 7) is named one of the top one hundred producers in the world.

The wines are equally distinguished. California's most famous grape, the zinfandel, arrived via emigrants from Kaštel, where it is still produced under the moniker 'kaštelanski crljenak'. The wines of central Dalmatia and the Šibenik coastline are famous the world over, especially those from the indigenous babič grape, along with tipples from the vineyards of Primošten. That such vintages can be created from this sparse soil is a tribute to the industry of the farmers. Dingač on the Pelješac peninsula yields Croatia's most lauded wine, alongside that from the islands of Korčula. If you want to know more, visit Hotel Boškinac in Novalje on Pag Island, or Hotel Vinarija in Slavonia; both run vineyards, wine workshops and fine kitchens.

Istria is famous for malvasija, thought to be one of the oldest grape types in existence, and the Familija Matijašić runs one of the region's leading vineyards. The area is also known for some of Croatia's richest cuisine. The famed truffle season starts in September and lasts for three months; a hunting excursion with dogs in the forests surrounding Motovun is a magical event. It's here that the largest truffle in the world was found. The truly truffle-lucky might snare a large white Tuber Magnico, which fetch upwards of £1,000 apiece.

The region abounds with restaurants dedicated to these earthy delicacies. Villa Annette hosts the president at suppertimes, while dinner at Valsabbion is a shining example of modern, seasonal Istrian cuisine.

Unlike some British restaurateurs, who jump on whichever gastronomic or environmental fad is popular at the time, Croatian cooks have a natural respect for organic production and ecological sensitivity. It is fascinating that, at a time when global cuisine is increasingly focusing on where food comes from and how it is prepared, Croatia's traditional approach should appear so modern.

The lambs of Pag, among the smallest in the world, produce some of Croatia's finest meat and cheese. As they graze on fields rich in medicinal herbs, their meat is ripe with essential oils. And since the fields are ruffled by the Bora wind, which carries vast quantities of salt up from the Adriatic,

the lambs' milk is turned into Croatia's most popular, naturally salted, cheese. The exceptional purity of the water around Ston has made it famous for its oysters, while farmers everywhere make an effort to work with the elements in order to maximise their produce.

If you want a deeper understanding of the traditional nature of Croatian agriculture, consider staying on an agroturizam. Many such places offer the opportunity for full involvement in farm life: milking cows, baking bread, picking grapes, riding horses. Croatian law stipulates that all the produce served at establishments labelled 'agrotouristic' must be entirely home-grown – from butter to wild boar, maraschino cherries to plum jams. Homesteads such as, Ravlić Agroturizam – an ancient wooden farm in Kratečko near Jasenovac – Pansion Marinka, a rustic guest house on Korčula, and Istria's Agroturizam Ograde are splendid choices for those looking to escape the pace of the city

Activities

Croatia's topography has just about every landscape the outdoors enthusiast could hope for. The National Parks are wonderful hiking territory and Cicerone publishes a great walking guide to Croatia: see www.cicerone.co.uk.

The adventurous can hang-glide or paraglide from Biokovo or Vidova Gora (on the mainland) to the island of Brač. Dalmatia's Elafiti and Kornati Islands have some of the best sea-kayaking around; you can also steer your modest craft under Dubrovnik's city walls. Raft and canoe safaris along the three rivers that run through Dalmatia's highlands are another possibility.

If you love riding then a farm stay could be ideal. The area surrounding Sinj near the Dalmatian highlands is

Photo www.istock.com

good horse riding country, with several stables accepting riders of all abilities. The Sunday group trot along the disused wine-train track from Karojba to Trieste is another special experience. Trajbar Team, Ranch Jelov Klanac and Eko-Selo Žumberak are three equestrian centres you will find within these pages.

There are great opportunities for rock climbing too, particularly in Paklenica National Park, with 400 routes. The wall stretching from Baška Voda to Makarska on Mount Biokovo has climbs between 200m and 400m; Brela, also on the Makarska riviera, has further breathtaking possibilities. The rocks surrounding Baška on Krk are satisfyingly rugged, as are those leading up from the watery valleys of the Dalmatian highlands, where free climbing is popular.

Scuba divers are in for a treat. Shipwrecks – notably that of the Baron Gautsch outside Rovinj and Dubrovnik's early-Roman remnants – and caves (those on the Kornati Islands are exceptional) are the primary focus for the coastline's innumerable diving agencies. Vis's past as a military base has preserved its marine life and is one of the few waterways that has not yet been plundered. The most commonly found sea life includes sardines, groupers, eels, snails sponges and sea fans. Coral reefs lie 40 metres down; Zlarin in the Šibenik region has a rich array of coral reefs, as does Mljet with its fine red coral. Krapanj has some of the best sea sponges. For more information go to www.diving.hr.

Yachtsmen love Croatia. For decades the Dalmatian coast has rivalled Mykonos, Marbella and the South of France as the best place to spot a £20m Sunseeker. With 40 marinas across the coast, even the tiniest enclaves have a place to moor your boat, though anything over three metres long requires a special permit to sail the Adriatic's deep channels – an idyllic way to explore the coastline and islands. The Adriatic Pilot is a book filled with invaluable information. www.imray.com, www.hgk.hr and www.aci-club.hr are useful web sites for nautical pursuits and marinas in Croatia.

Photo Ivo Pervan, Croatian Tourist Board

Croatia's National Parks cover an astounding 7.5% of the country's landmass, and offer eight abundantly varied topographies to climb, sail, hike, ride and cycle through.

Tito's summer residence and a resort since the late 19th century, the Brijuni archipelago (www.np-brijuni.hr) is the only National Park in Istria. Comprising two vast and 12 smaller islands, this may not be an example of nature at its most untamed, but it does provide a captivating day out with fabulous diving opportunities. Like a natural-history theme park, the landscape, with its deer, mouflon, 1,000-year-old olive trees, Roman excavations and dinosaur footprints, can be discovered on an organised tour or freestyle by golf cart.

Whispered to be the most underrated of the parks, Risnjak spans the Gorski Kotar mountains, descending from Slovenia right through to northern Rijeka, with winter sports, the beautiful Leska trail and fewer tourist trappings than its counterparts.

Paklenica National Park, meanwhile, provides one of the richest rock-climbing backdrops. Striking karst gorges, cliffs, caves and grottos hide a magnetic selection of stalactites and stalagmites. Lucky visitors might spot the legendary griffon, for this is one of just two Croatian sites the mighty vultures call home.

The waterfalls of Plitvice Lakes are perhaps the best-known feature of Croatia's National Parks. A UNESCO World Heritage site with a sequence of 16 cascades, the lakes are surrounded by dense forests inhabited by bears, wolves and wild boars.

The river springing from the foot of the Dinara Mountain, winding through to Šibenik's shore, gives way to the extraordinary Krka Falls. Flowing over travertine barriers and deep canyons, it encompasses a sequence of waterfalls, the Skradinski Buk the most bewitching of them all; nearby, the Visovac Lake holds an islet with a Franciscan monastery and church while elsewhere lie functioning watermills.

The Kornati Islands in the Zadar archipelago consist of 140 islets, reefs, rocks and islands, 89 of which are declared a National Park. Largely barren – of both humans and vegetation – the other-worldly rock formations are a highlight of the Dalmatian coastline. Blue cliff faces extend hundreds of metres over taupe seas, near hidden beaches, coves and bays, while wild

mouflon mountain sheep add their own untamed note.

Looking onto Kornati, Northern Velebit National Park's patchwork of forest-covered mountains, foothills, ravines and ridges encompass a UNESCO-declared World Biosphere Reserve of karst rock. Among the

Photo Milan Babič, Croatian Tourist Board

zigzagging mountaineering trails is the Premužić, weaving through the park's most splendid terrains and sights. Ruins are dotted throughout, a testament to populations long gone, while views extend over the neighbouring islands.

A third of the island of Mljet, one of the Adriatic's most beautiful islands, is a designated National Park. It's thought that Odysseus was held captive on Mljet by Calypso, and it's hard to imagine why anyone would wish to leave. This most southerly National Park contains a 12th-century Benedictine monastery, saltwater lakes surrounded by lush vegetation, and Indian mongooses - introduced in 1909 to purge the island of its burgeoning community of snakes.

Photo Ivo Pervan, Croatian Tourist Board

Heroes and villains

Croatia has epic associations, its earliest history touched by legend. Jason sought refuge with Medea and his Golden Fleece on Kvarner's Apsyrtides Islands, while Diomedes, a Greek warrior who survived the Trojan war, is said to be buried on the island that most intrigued him, Palagruža. The local birds are the souls of his dead warriors, sent by Zeus to protect his grave.

Croatia's supernatural descendants live on today. Fable decrees that the world's witches and elves gather in Klek at midnight on stormy nights, while the Vodnjan mummies – the bodies of 16th-century saints – have, mysteriously, defied science and never decomposed.

Istria has some strong literary connections. Part of Dante's Divine Comedy is set in Pula, the town where James Joyce famously spent time with his wife teaching English in 1906. Casanova took home fond memories of Vrsar – both its wine and its women – while the Pazin Pit was made famous by Jules Verne. George Bernard Shaw, on the other hand, fell in love with Dalmatia, declaring that: "On the last day of Creation God desired to crown His work, and thus created the Kornati Islands out of tears, stars and breath."

Croatia has its share of inventors and travellers, either through birth or domicile. Marco Polo allegedly came from Korčula, Faust Vrančić – the inventor of the parachute – came from Sisak, and Robert Koch successfully fought malaria on the Brijuni Islands. And we can stretch a point to include the army alongside these creative Croatians, since the not-so-humble cravat started life as part of the uniform worn by Ferdinand II's soldiers in the Thirty Years' War (1618-1648). Perhaps these soldiers learned about stereotype-defying behaviour from 16th-century Uskosk pirates, who campaigned for tillable land. Their trial revealed that, of the nine Englishmen in the group, six were of noble birth.

Photo www.istock.com

Our offices

Beautiful as they were, our old offices leaked heat, used electricity to heat water and rooms, flooded whole rooms with light to illuminate one person, and were not ours to alter. We failed our eco-audit in spite of using recycled cooking oil in one car and gas in another, recycling everything we could and gently promoting 'greenery' in our travel books. (Our Fragile Earth series takes a harder line.)

After two eco-audits we leaped at the chance to buy some old barns closer to Bristol, to create our own eco-offices and start again. Our accountants thought we were mad and there was no time for proper budgeting. The back of every envelope bore the signs of frenzied calculations, and then I shook hands and went off on holiday.

Two years later we moved in.

As I write, swallows are nesting in our wood-pellet store, the fountain plays in the pond, the grasses bend before a gentle breeze and the solar panels heat water too hot to touch. We have, to our delight, created an inspiring and serene place.

The roof was lifted to allow us to fix thick insulation panels beneath the tiles. More panels were fitted between the rafters and as a separate wall inside the old ones, and laid under the under floor heating pipes. We are insulated for the Arctic, and almost totally air-tight. Ventilation is natural, and we open windows. An Austrian boiler sucks wood-pellets in from an outside store and slowly consumes them, cleanly and – of course – without using any fossil fuels. Rain-water is channelled to a 6,000-litre underground tank and then, filtered, flushes loos and fills basins. Sun-pipes funnel the daylight into dark corners and double-glazed Velux windows, most facing north, pour it into every office.

Photos above Quentin Craven

We built a small green-oak barn between two old barns, and this has become the heart of the offices, warm, light and beautiful. Wood plays a major role: our simple oak desks were made by a local carpenter, my office floor is of oak, and there is oak panelling. Even the carpet tiles tell a story; they are made from the wool of Herdwick sheep from the Lake District.

Our electricity consumption is extraordinarily low. We set out not to flood the buildings with light, but to provide attractive, low background lighting and individual 'task' lights to be used only as needed. Materials, too, have been a focus: we used non-toxic paints and finishes.

Events blew our budgets apart, but we have a building of which we are proud and which has helped us win two national awards this year. Architects and designers are fascinated and we are all working with a renewed commitment. But, best of all, we are now in a better position to encourage our 'owners' and readers to take 'sustainability' more seriously.

I end by answering an obvious question: our office carbon emissions will be reduced by about 75%. We await our bills, but they will be low and, as time goes by, relatively lower – and lower. It has been worth every penny and every ounce of effort.

Alastair Sawday

Photo above www.paulgroom.com
Photo below Tom Germain

ALASTAIR SAWDAY'S
SPECIAL ESCAPES

Home • Search • Hotlist • Owners • Links

The Flat, Sloane Square

London, England

You're in the heart of town, yet tucked up in a smart residential street. Sloane Square tube is on your doorstep, you can be on the King's Road within three minutes and the No. 19 bus whisks you off to Knightsbridge and beyond. The apartment is dreamy; you will linger in the morning, then find an excuse to bolt home in the afternoon. Climb up to the third floor to discover an enormous glass roof flooding the hall with light. Glittering elegance comes in the form of Farrow & Ball paints, a 1793 Chatelet great-grandfather clock, a walnut dining table, a gilded Venetian bedhead and halogen lights. The sofa, covered in raw silk, was too big to come through the door so the delivery man pulled it up single-handedly, tottering on the tiny balcony. Best of all is the exquisite art that hangs on the walls (Frederique represents several artists and holds shows in New York). A super-comfy double bed wears crisp Egyptian cotton, a leaf from a Burmese bible graces the sitting room wall and a mellow marble bathroom pampers. The kitchen is similarly resplendent with dishwasher, hanging pots and stainless steel oven. Exceptional.

Sloane Gardens.

Details for The Flat

Contact Frederique Browne	sleeps:
tel: 020 7823 4704	rooms: 2: 1 double, 1 single, sharing bathroom.
@ Send E-mail Enquiry	price: £0 – £850.
)) Visit Web Site	closed: Never.
	changeover: Flexible.

? Details Explanation

€ Currency Converter

? Symbol Explanations

Hall.

Living area in Flat 4.

Why Come Here?

Checklist

✓ Dishwasher
✓ Electricity included
✓ Washing machine

✓ Television
✓ Land line telephone**
✓ Restaurant nearby
✓ Iron & ironing board
✓ Public transport
✓ Music system***

** May only be for incoming calls
*** Not necessarily including CD player

More details here »

Points Of Interest

○ Two minutes away from Royal Court Theatre.
○ Near to Peter Jones department store.
○ Battersea Park a 10-minute walk away.
○ 5 minutes from the river and the Chelsea Flower Show.

This information is provided by owners and is not endorsed by ASP. If you have questions about it, please contact the owners.

Master bedroom in Flat 4.

Now what?

○ Add The Flat to your Hotlist »
○ Find other Special Escapes in London »
○ Booking Advice for Special Escapes »

Cosy cottages • Sumptuous castles • City apartments
• Hilltop bothies • Tipis and more

A whole week self-catering in Britain with your friends or family is precious, and you dare not get it wrong. To whom do you turn for advice and who on earth do you trust when the web is awash with advice from strangers? We launched Special Escapes to satisfy an obvious need for impartial and trustworthy help – and that is what it provides. The criteria for inclusion are the same as for our books: we have to like the place and the owners. It has, quite simply, to be 'special'. The site, our first online-only publication, is featured on www.thegoodwebguide.com and is growing fast.

www.specialescapes.co.uk

Where on the web?

The World Wide Web is big – very big. So big, in fact, that it can be a fruitless search if you don't know where to find reliable, trustworthy, up-to-date information about fantastic places to stay in Europe, India, Morocco and beyond...

Fortunately, there's www.specialplacestostay.com, where you can dip into all of our guides, find special offers from owners, catch up on news about the series and tell us about the special places you've been to.

www.specialplacestostay.com

The Little Food Book   Edition 1, £6.99

By Craig Sams, Chairman of the Soil Association

An explosive account of the food we eat today. Never have we been at such risk –
from our food. This book will help clarify what's at stake.

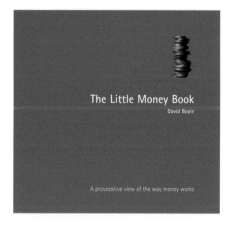

The Little Money Book   Edition 1, £6.99

By David Boyle, an associate of the New Economics Foundation

This pithy, wry little guide will tell you where money comes from, what it means,
what it's doing to the planet and what we might be able to do about it.

www.fragile-earth.com

One Planet Living

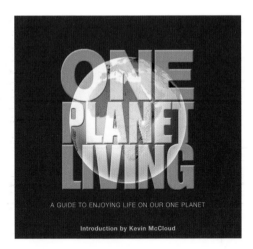

One Planet Living is a practical guide providing us with easy, affordable and attractive alternatives for achieving a higher quality of life while using our fair share of the planet's capacity. Two environmental organisations, BioRegional and WWF, have come together to promote a simple set of principles to make sustainable living achievable:

- Zero carbon – how to reduce our dependence on fossil fuels by supporting renewables
- Natural habitats and wildlife – how to reconnect with the natural world around us
- Local and sustainable food – temper our desire for strawberries in January and go for local, organic and seasonal instead
- Sustainable water – simple ways of cutting back on water consumption, because every drop counts
- Sustainable transport – shifting our reliance on planes and car journeys, and suggesting enjoyable alternatives
- Culture and heritage – how a sense of identity contributes towards our legacy
- Zero waste – reduce, repair, re-use, recycle and buy recycled
- Equity and fair trade – supporting local development and decent prices for all traders
- Sustainable materials – how buying recycled or sustainable products can protect and enhance our natural world
- Health and happiness – go for the simple things in life and feel better for it

This inspiring little book with a foreword by Kevin McCloud takes each of these principles and shows the reader how to embrace and apply them to their everyday lives.

£4.99 – small change for big change

Six Days

Celebrating the triumph of creativity over adversity.

An inspiring and heart-rending story of the making of the stained-glass 'Creation' window at Chester Cathedral by a woman battling with debilitating Parkinson's disease.

"Within a few seconds, the tears were running down my cheeks. The window was one of the most beautiful things I had ever seen. It is a tour-de force, playing with light like no other window ..."
Anthropologist Hugh Brody

In 1983, Ros Grimshaw, a distinguished designer, artist and creator of stained-glass windows, was diagnosed with Parkinson's disease. Refusing to allow her illness to prevent her from working, Ros became even more adept at her craft, and in 2000 won the commission to design and make the 'Creation' Stained Glass Window for Chester Cathedral.

Six Days traces the evolution of the window from the first sketches to its final, glorious completion as a rare and wonderful tribute to Life itself: for each of the six 'days' of Creation recounted in Genesis, there is a scene below that is relevant to the world of today and tomorrow.

Heart-rending extracts from Ros's diary capture the personal struggle involved. Superb photography captures the luminescence of the stunning stained glass, while the story weaves together essays, poems, and moving contributions from Ros's partner, Patrick Costeloe.

Available from Alastair Sawday Publishing £12.99

Order form

All these books are available in major bookshops or you may order them direct.
Post and packaging are FREE within the UK.

Bed & Breakfast for Garden Lovers	£14.99
British Hotels, Inns & Other Places	£14.99
British Bed & Breakfast	£14.99
French Bed & Breakfast	£15.99
French Hotels, Châteaux & Other Places	£14.99
French Holiday Homes	£12.99
Green Places to Stay	**£13.99**
Greece	£11.99
India	£11.99
Ireland	£12.99
Italy	£14.99
London	£9.99
Morocco	£11.99
Mountains of Europe	£9.99
Paris Hotels	£9.99
Portugal	£10.99
Pubs & Inns of England & Wales	£13.99
Spain	£14.99
Turkey	£11.99
The Little Food Book	£6.99
The Little Money Book	£6.99
One Planet Living	£4.99
Six Days	£12.99

Please make cheques payable to Alastair Sawday Publishing	Total £

Please send cheques to: Alastair Sawday Publishing, The Old Farmyard, Yanley
Lane, Long Ashton, Bristol BS41 9LR. For credit card orders call 01275 395431
or order directly from our web site www.specialplacestostay.com

Title   First name   Surname

Address

Postcode   Tel   CR01

If you do not wish to receive mail from other like-minded companies, please tick here ☐
If you would prefer not to receive information about special offers on our books, please tick here ☐

Report form

If you have any comments on entries in this guide, please let us have them. If you have a favourite house, hotel, inn or other new discovery, please let us know about it. You can return this form, email info@sawdays.co.uk, or visit www.specialplacestostay.com and click on 'contact'.

Existing entry
Property name: _____

Entry number: _____ Date of visit: ___ / ___ / ___

New recommendation
Property name: _____

Address: _____

_____

Tel: _____

Your comments
What did you like (or dislike) about this place? Were the people friendly? What was the location like? What sort of food did they serve?

_____
_____
_____
_____
_____
_____
_____
_____

Your details
Name: _____

Address: _____

Postcode: _____ Tel: _____

CR01

Please send completed form to ASP, The Old Farmyard, Yanley Lane, Long Ashton, Bristol BS41 9LR

Wheelchair-accessible

These places have full wheelchair facilities.

Istria 5 • 8 • 15
Kvarner 56 • 64 • 68
North & Central Dalmatia 99
South Dalmatia 124
Zagreb & the interior 145 • 148 • 149

Budget

These places have double rooms for £70 (€100) or under.

Istria 3 • 4 • 6 • 7 • 10 • 11 • 12 • 15 • 16 • 17 • 18 • 19 • 21 • 22 • 24 • 25 • 29 • 34 • 35 • 36 • 37 • 39 • 40 • 41 • 42 • 44 • 46 • 47 • 48 • 49 • 52
Kvarner 60 • 61 • 62 • 63 • 65 • 67 • 71
North & Central Dalmatia 76 • 77 • 79 • 80 • 82 • 83 • 86 • 87 • 101 • 103
South Dalmatia 107 • 109 • 110 • 111 • 112 • 114 • 116 • 118 • 119 • 121 • 124 • 127 • 128 • 129 • 130 • 131 • 134 • 135 • 136 • 138 • 139 • 142
Zagreb & the interior 144 • 146 • 147 • 150 • 151 • 152 • 153 • 154 • 156 • 157 • 158 • 160 • 161

Singles

These places either have a single room or charge no single supplement.
Istria 10 • 11 • 18 • 19 • 32

• 39 • 40
Kvarner 55 • 63
North & Central Dalmatia 73 • 77 • 79 • 85 • 104
South Dalmatia 106 • 110 • 118 • 119 • 127 • 128
Zagreb & the interior 143 • 147 • 151 • 154 • 157 • 158 • 159 • 160 • 161

Public transport

These properties have regular public transport stops within 500m, or owner collects from public transport stop.

Istria 5 • 7 • 12 • 15 • 17 • 18 • 21 • 22 • 24 • 26 • 27 • 28 • 29 • 32 • 33 • 34 • 35 • 39 • 40 • 42 • 46 • 47 • 48 • 51 • 54
Kvarner 55 • 56 • 57 • 58 • 60 • 64 • 66 • 68 • 69
North & Central Dalmatia 73 • 75 • 76 • 77 • 79 • 80 • 81 • 82 • 83 • 84 • 85 • 86 • 87 • 88 • 89 • 90 • 92 • 93 • 94 • 95 • 96 • 97 • 98 • 99 • 101 • 103
South Dalmatia 106 • 107 • 108 • 109 • 110 • 111 • 112 • 116 • 117 • 118 • 119 • 120 • 121 • 122 • 123 • 124 • 126 • 127 • 128 • 129 • 130 • 131 • 132 • 133 • 134 • 135 • 136 • 137 • 138 • 139 • 140 • 141 • 142
Zagreb & the interior 143 • 144 • 145 • 147 • 148 • 149 • 150 • 151 • 152 •

Beach
These places are on or near a beach within strolling distance.

Environmentally-friendly

These places have at least two of the following: solar energy, water recycling, own organic food, only natural materials used; plus a genuine ecological conscience.

Family room

Home grown food

Quick reference indices

Index by property name

Index by place

Photo Ravlić, entry 158

How to use this book

South Dalmatia **1**

Villa Mediterane
Viganj 224, Kućište, 20267 Dubrovnik-Neretva

2 Fishermen's houses line the harbour wall of the sleepy resort of Orebić, and the streets are dotted with cypresses and pines. A string of foliage-backed beaches stretches northwest to Viganj – and the Villa Mediterane sitting unobtrusively on the shore. Palms and pines part to reveal a gleaming white, modernist exterior, plus two swimming pools circled by sun umbrellas and recliners. Windsurfers play off the hotel beach, exploiting the Maestral winds; the less energetic are to be found dipping their toes in the surf. Rooms have been styled with an unexpected spontaneity, their wooden floors and painted wooden furniture creating the feel of a Key West hotel. Delightful staff devote themselves to looking after you, and this is a great place for families, with several self-catering apartments and plenty of safe spots outdoors. Meals promise local ingredients and Croatian wines: reds from Orebić, whites from across the channel in Korčula. It's a marvellous little place and with a car you can explore all those fishing villages along the Pelješac peninsula. *Minimum stay three nights July/August. Bikes available for hire.*

3	rooms	12 + 11: 12 doubles. 11 apartments for 2-4.
4	price	€40-€70. Singles less 20%. Half-board €30-€45 p.p. Apartments €40-€85. Prices per night.
5	meals	Dinner €13.
6	closed	November-March.
7	directions	From Orebić, 8km northwest along coast. Detailed directions on booking.

Tomislav Ančić

tel	+385 (0)20 719 096
mobile	+385 (0)91 615 5003
fax	+385 (0)20 719 106
email	korcula-bus@du.htnet.hr
web	www.villa-mediterane.com

Hotel & Self-catering **8**

 **10**

Map 7 Entry 106 **9**